Gates of Prayer for Shabbat

שַׁעֲרֵי תְּפִלָּה
לְשַׁבָּת

A Gender Sensitive Prayerbook

Chaim Stern, Editor

CENTRAL CONFERENCE OF AMERICAN RABBIS
1992

The Central Conference of American Rabbis
expresses its sincere appreciation to
James Nathaniel Dreyfus
and
Richard Baeck Dreyfus
whose contribution has made possible
this publication of
Gates of Prayer for Shabbat
in honor of their father

RABBI A. STANLEY DREYFUS

Contents

Library of Congress Cataloging-in-Publication Data

Siddur (Reform, Central Conference of American Rabbis). Sabbath.
  English & Hebrew.
    [Sha'are tefilah] = Gates of prayer for Shabbat / Chaim Stern,
  editor — Gender-neutral ed.
        p.   cm.
    English and Hebrew.
    ISBN 0-88123-032-4 (Eng. opening) —
    ISBN 0-88123-033-2 (Heb. opening)
    1. Sabbath—Liturgy—Texts.   2. Siddurim—Texts.   3. Reform
  Judaism—Liturgy—Texts.   4. Sexism in liturgical language.
  I. Stern, Chaim.   II. Title.   III. Title: Gates of prayer for Shabbat.
  BM675.S3Z663413   1992
  296.4'1—dc20   91-38484
                                                           CIP
                                                            HE

Designed by Chaim Stern with Barry Nostradamus Sher. Typography by El Ot, Tel Aviv.

Preface

Just before *Gates of Prayer* went to press in late 1974, the editor changed all English-language references to human beings in general that on their face excluded women, to gender-neutral terms. Thus, 'mankind' became 'humankind,' 'fathers' became 'ancestors' or 'fathers and mothers,' and so on. He did not at that time change language referring to God and he made no attempt to emend the Hebrew texts. Now, sixteen years later, we present several services for Shabbat in which the gender-neutral approach is extended to English-language references to God, and, in some small degree to the Hebrew.

There are few tasks in liturgy more challenging than the one currently under discussion in the Reform Movement and in other branches of Judaism, both in North America and elsewhere: how to respond to the need, felt by many, to reshape the language of our liturgy so that it will reflect our view that masculine language and exclusively male assumptions ought to give way to broader, more inclusive expression.

We hope the present volume may be a contribution towards that end.

We thank the many colleagues whose helpful suggestions and criticisms have been gratefully received and carefully considered. This Edition would have been the poorer without their help. Rabbi H. Leonard Poller, Rabbi Donna Berman, and Cantor Edward Graham formed, with the Editor, a working group that studied the Editor's final draft, and helped decide on many matters. To them, a particular word of thanks.

Chaim Stern
CHAPPAQUA, NEW YORK

On Usage

We utilize a number of conventions in this prayer book, which we suggest you note carefully.

☞ The type-style of this paragraph is used whenever we suggest the English be read by the person leading the service.

> ☞ *The oblique style of this paragraph is used whenever we suggest that the congregation as a whole might read the English. In addition, passages in this type-style are indented. In those congregations where unison reading is not the norm, this type-style might identify passages to be read by diverse individuals.*

☞ Following the convention established in Gates of Prayer, this sans-serif type-style suggests passages (usually but not exclusively Hebrew) which might be chanted or sung. Please note that any other passages may be chanted or sung. Of course, not all such passages will likely be chanted in a given service.

In several services the English accompanying some Hebrew passages does not translate that Hebrew. We utilize two symbols to inform the worshipper who is not adequately Hebrew-literate to know this without help:

° This signifies that the English is a variation on the theme of the Hebrew. Hewing to the theme of the Hebrew, the English may come to that theme from a (sometimes very) different perspective.

* This signifies that the English is a paraphrase of the Hebrew. You will find this symbol in the morning service, where the English is often an abbreviated paraphrase of the preceding Hebrew.

Shabbat Evening Service I

(For congregations where the lights are kindled in the synagogue)

הדלקת הנרות

אֵל הָרַחֲמִים, אָנָּא מְשׁךְ חַסְדְּךָ עָלֵינוּ וְעַל קְרוֹבֵינוּ הָאֲהוּבִים. וְזַכֵּנוּ
לָלֶכֶת בְּדַרְכֵי יְשָׁרִים לְפָנֶיךָ, דְּבֵקִים בַּתּוֹרָה וּבְמַעֲשִׂים טוֹבִים.

Source of mercy, continue Your loving care for us and our loved
ones. Give us strength to walk in Your presence on the paths of
the righteous, loyal to Your Torah, steadfast in goodness.

וְהַרְחֵק מֵעָלֵינוּ כָּל־חֶרְפָּה, תּוּגָה, וְיָגוֹן. וְשִׂים שָׁלוֹם, אוֹרָה,
וְשִׂמְחָה בִּמְעוֹנֵנוּ. כִּי עִמְּךָ מְקוֹר הַחַיִּים. בְּאוֹרְךָ נִרְאֶה אוֹר. אָמֵן.

Keep us far from all shame, grief, and anguish; fill our homes with
peace, light, and joy. O God, fountain of life, by Your light do we
see light.

❖ ❖

בָּרוּךְ אַתָּה יְיָ, אֱלֹהֵינוּ מֶלֶךְ הָעוֹלָם, אֲשֶׁר קִדְּשָׁנוּ
בְּמִצְוֹתָיו וְצִוָּנוּ לְהַדְלִיק נֵר שֶׁל שַׁבָּת.

Ba-ruch a-ta Adonai, Eh-lo-hei-nu meh-lech ha-o-lam, ah-sher
kid'sha-nu b'mitz-vo-tav, v'tzi-va-nu l'had-lik ner shel Shabbat.

Praised be our Eternal God, Ruler of the universe: You hallow us
with Mitzvot, and command us to kindle the lights of Shabbat.

May God bless us with Shabbat joy.
May God bless us with Shabbat holiness.
May God bless us with Shabbat peace.

1

Shabbat Evening Service I

Welcoming Shabbat   קבלת שבת

(One or more of the following passages may be read or chanted)

From Psalm 95

לְכוּ נְרַנְּנָה לַיהוָה, נָרִיעָה לְצוּר יִשְׁעֵנוּ.

נְקַדְּמָה פָנָיו בְּתוֹדָה, בִּזְמִרוֹת נָרִיעַ לוֹ.

כִּי אֵל גָּדוֹל יְהוָה וּמֶלֶךְ גָּדוֹל עַל־כָּל־אֱלֹהִים.

אֲשֶׁר בְּיָדוֹ מֶחְקְרֵי־אָרֶץ, וְתוֹעֲפוֹת הָרִים לוֹ.

אֲשֶׁר־לוֹ הַיָּם, וְהוּא עָשָׂהוּ, וְיַבֶּשֶׁת יָדָיו יָצָרוּ.

כִּי הוּא אֱלֹהֵינוּ, וַאֲנַחְנוּ עַם מַרְעִיתוֹ וְצֹאן יָדוֹ:

הַיּוֹם אִם־בְּקֹלוֹ תִשְׁמָעוּ!

Come, let us sing to the Eternal One,
> *let our song ring out to our sheltering Rock.*

Let us come before God with thanksgiving,
> *our voices loud with song.*

For great are You, Eternal One,
> *high above the gods that are worshipped.*

In Your hands are the depths of the earth;
> *Yours are the mountain-peaks.*

You made the sea, it is Yours;
> *the dry land is the work of Your hands.*

You are our God and our Shepherd;
> *we are Your people and Your flock:*

If only today we would listen to Your voice!

From Psalm 96

שִׁירוּ לַיהוָה שִׁיר חָדָשׁ; שִׁירוּ לַיהוָה כָּל־הָאָרֶץ!
שִׁירוּ לַיהוָה, בָּרְכוּ שְׁמוֹ; בַּשְּׂרוּ מִיּוֹם־לְיוֹם יְשׁוּעָתוֹ.

Sing a new song to God;
all the earth sing to the Eternal One!

Sing to the Eternal One, praise God's name,
tell of God's power from day to day.

סַפְּרוּ בַגּוֹיִם כְּבוֹדוֹ, בְּכָל־הָעַמִּים נִפְלְאוֹתָיו.
כִּי גָדוֹל יְהוָה, וּמְהֻלָּל מְאֹד, נוֹרָא הוּא עַל־כָּל־אֱלֹהִים.

Declare God's glory among the nations,
God's wonders among the peoples.

For great is the Eternal One, beyond all praise,
and awesome, far above the gods that are worshipped!

כִּי כָּל־אֱלֹהֵי הָעַמִּים אֱלִילִים, וַיהוָה שָׁמַיִם עָשָׂה.
הוֹד־וְהָדָר לְפָנָיו, עֹז וְתִפְאֶרֶת בְּמִקְדָּשׁוֹ.

The other gods are but idols:
the Eternal One made the heavens.

Honor and beauty attend You,
strength and splendor are in Your presence.

הָבוּ לַיהוָה, מִשְׁפְּחוֹת עַמִּים, הָבוּ לַיהוָה כָּבוֹד וָעֹז.
הָבוּ לַיהוָה כְּבוֹד שְׁמוֹ; הִשְׁתַּחֲווּ לַיהוָה בְּהַדְרַת־קֹדֶשׁ.

Honor the Eternal One, all races and peoples,
Acknowledge the Eternal One's glory and might.

Honor the Eternal One's glory;
worship your God in the beauty of holiness.

חִילוּ מִפָּנָיו כָּל־הָאָרֶץ. אִמְרוּ בַגּוֹיִם: יְהֹוָה מָלָךְ;
אַף־תִּכּוֹן תֵּבֵל, בַּל־תִּמּוֹט: יָדִין עַמִּים בְּמֵישָׁרִים.
יִשְׂמְחוּ הַשָּׁמַיִם וְתָגֵל הָאָרֶץ; יִרְעַם הַיָּם וּמְלֹאוֹ.

Let all the earth tremble at God's presence.
Declare to the nations: God reigns;

> *now the world is secure and firmly based;*
> *God rules the peoples with justice.*

Let the heavens be glad and the earth rejoice;

> *let the sea roar, and all that fills it.*

יַעֲלֹז שָׂדַי וְכָל־אֲשֶׁר־בּוֹ;
אָז יְרַנְּנוּ כָּל־עֲצֵי־יָעַר לִפְנֵי יְהֹוָה.
כִּי בָא, כִּי בָא לִשְׁפֹּט הָאָרֶץ:

Let the field and its creatures exult;

> *let the trees of the forest sing for joy before God,*
> *who comes to rule the earth:*

יִשְׁפֹּט־תֵּבֵל בְּצֶדֶק, וְעַמִּים בֶּאֱמוּנָתוֹ.

to rule the world with justice,

> *to rule the peoples with truth.*

From Psalm 97

יְהֹוָה מָלָךְ: תָּגֵל הָאָרֶץ, יִשְׂמְחוּ אִיִּים רַבִּים.
עָנָן וַעֲרָפֶל סְבִיבָיו; צֶדֶק וּמִשְׁפָּט מְכוֹן כִּסְאוֹ.

The Eternal One reigns: let the earth rejoice,

> *let the many isles be glad.*

Cloud and mist surround You,

> *right and justice are the foundation of Your throne.*

הַגִּֽידוּ הַשָּׁמַֽיִם צִדְקוֹ, וְרָאוּ כָל־הָעַמִּים כְּבוֹדוֹ.
שָׁמְעָה וַתִּשְׂמַח צִיּוֹן; וַתָּגֵֽלְנָה בְּנוֹת יְהוּדָה,
לְמַֽעַן מִשְׁפָּטֶֽיךָ, יְהֹוָה.

The heavens tell of Your righteousness;
the peoples witness Your glory.

Zion hears and is glad;
the cities of Judah rejoice, Eternal One,
over Your judgments.

כִּי־אַתָּה, יְהֹוָה, עֶלְיוֹן עַל־כָּל־הָאָֽרֶץ:
מְאֹד נַעֲלֵֽיתָ עַל־כָּל־אֱלֹהִים.

For You are supreme over all the earth,
You are exalted far above the gods that are worshipped.

אוֹר זָרֻֽעַ לַצַּדִּיק, וּלְיִשְׁרֵי־לֵב שִׂמְחָה.

Light dawns for the righteous,
gladness for the upright in heart.

שִׂמְחוּ צַדִּיקִים בַּיהֹוָה, וְהוֹדוּ לְזֵֽכֶר קָדְשׁוֹ.

Let the righteous rejoice in You,
and give thanks to Your holy name.

From Psalm 98

מִזְמוֹר. שִֽׁירוּ לַיהֹוָה שִׁיר חָדָשׁ, כִּי־נִפְלָאוֹת עָשָׂה.
הוֹדִֽיעַ יְהֹוָה יְשׁוּעָתוֹ; לְעֵינֵי הַגּוֹיִם גִּלָּה צִדְקָתוֹ.

Sing a new song to the Eternal One, who has done wonders:
You have made known Your power,
and revealed Your justice for all to see.

5

זָכַר חַסְדּוֹ וֶאֱמוּנָתוֹ לְבֵית יִשְׂרָאֵל.

רָאוּ כָל־אַפְסֵי־אָרֶץ אֵת יְשׁוּעַת אֱלֹהֵינוּ.

You have remembered Your love and faithfulness to Israel.

All the ends of the earth have seen the power of God.

הָרִיעוּ לַיהוָה כָּל־הָאָרֶץ; פִּצְחוּ וְרַנְּנוּ וְזַמֵּרוּ!

בַּחֲצֹצְרוֹת וְקוֹל שׁוֹפָר הָרִיעוּ לִפְנֵי הַמֶּלֶךְ יְהוָה.

Let the earth ring out in song to God;
break forth, sing aloud, shout praise!

Sound trumpet and horn
before the sovereign God.

יִרְעַם הַיָּם וּמְלֹאוֹ; תֵּבֵל וְיֹשְׁבֵי בָהּ.

נְהָרוֹת יִמְחֲאוּ־כָף! יַחַד הָרִים יְרַנֵּנוּ לִפְנֵי־יְהוָה,

כִּי בָא לִשְׁפֹּט הָאָרֶץ:

Let the sea roar, and all that fills it,

the world, and all who dwell there.

Let the rivers clap hands!

Let the mountains sing for joy before God,
who comes to rule the earth:

יִשְׁפֹּט־תֵּבֵל בְּצֶדֶק, וְעַמִּים בְּמֵישָׁרִים.

to rule the world with justice,

and the peoples with righteousness.

From Psalm 99

יְהוָה מָלָךְ: יִרְגְּזוּ עַמִּים. יֹשֵׁב כְּרוּבִים, תָּנוּט הָאָרֶץ.

יְהוָה בְּצִיּוֹן גָּדוֹל, וְרָם הוּא עַל־כָּל־הָעַמִּים.

יוֹדוּ שִׁמְךָ: גָּדוֹל וְנוֹרָא, קָדוֹשׁ הוּא.

וְעֹז מֶלֶךְ, מִשְׁפָּט אָהֵב: אַתָּה כּוֹנַנְתָּ מֵישָׁרִים,
מִשְׁפָּט וּצְדָקָה בְּיַעֲקֹב אַתָּה עָשִׂיתָ. רוֹמְמוּ יְהֹוָה אֱלֹהֵינוּ,
וְהִשְׁתַּחֲווּ לַהֲדֹם רַגְלָיו קָדוֹשׁ הוּא. רוֹמְמוּ יְהֹוָה אֱלֹהֵינוּ,
וְהִשְׁתַּחֲווּ לְהַר קָדְשׁוֹ, כִּי־קָדוֹשׁ יְהֹוָה אֱלֹהֵינוּ.

The Eternal One reigns: let the peoples quake with awe; God sits
enthroned, and the earth trembles. You are exalted in Zion,
Eternal One, high above the peoples. Let them praise Your name,
great and awesome and holy. Your power, 0 Sovereign God, is in
Your love of justice. You make righteousness stand firm; justice
and right take root in Jacob. We will exalt You, our Eternal God,
and worship at Your holy mountain, for our Eternal God is holy.

Psalm 29

מִזְמוֹר לְדָוִד.

הָבוּ לַיהֹוָה, בְּנֵי אֵלִים, הָבוּ לַיהֹוָה כָּבוֹד וָעֹז!

הָבוּ לַיהֹוָה כְּבוֹד שְׁמוֹ, הִשְׁתַּחֲווּ לַיהֹוָה בְּהַדְרַת־קֹדֶשׁ.

A Song of David.
Ascribe to the Eternal One, all celestial beings, honor and strength!
Praise the Eternal One, whose name is great; worship your God in
the beauty of holiness.

קוֹל יְהֹוָה עַל־הַמָּיִם! אֵל־הַכָּבוֹד הִרְעִים! יְהֹוָה עַל־מַיִם רַבִּים!

קוֹל־יְהֹוָה בַּכֹּחַ, קוֹל יְהֹוָה בֶּהָדָר,

קוֹל יְהֹוָה שֹׁבֵר אֲרָזִים, וַיְשַׁבֵּר יְהֹוָה אֶת־אַרְזֵי הַלְּבָנוֹן.

וַיַּרְקִידֵם כְּמוֹ־עֵגֶל לְבָנוֹן וְשִׂרְיֹן כְּמוֹ בֶן־רְאֵמִים.

The Eternal One's voice above the waters! The God of glory
thunders! The Eternal One's voice, with power—the Eternal One's
voice, majestic—the Eternal One's voice breaks cedars; God
shatters Lebanon's cedars, making Lebanon skip like a calf, Sirion
like a wild young ox.

קוֹל־יְהוָה חֹצֵב לַהֲבוֹת אֵשׁ;

קוֹל יְהוָה יָחִיל מִדְבָּר; יָחִיל יְהוָה מִדְבַּר קָדֵשׁ;

קוֹל יְהוָה יְחוֹלֵל אַיָּלוֹת, וַיֶּחֱשֹׂף יְעָרוֹת,

וּבְהֵיכָלוֹ כֻּלּוֹ אֹמֵר: כָּבוֹד!

Eternal God! Your voice sparks fiery flames; Eternal God! Your voice makes the desert spin; Eternal God! Your voice shakes the Kadesh desert; Eternal God! Your voice uproots the oaks, and strips the forests bare, while in Your temple all cry: 'Glory!'

יְהוָה לַמַּבּוּל יָשָׁב, וַיֵּשֶׁב יְהוָה מֶלֶךְ לְעוֹלָם.

יְהוָה עֹז לְעַמּוֹ יִתֵּן, יְהוָה יְבָרֵךְ אֶת־עַמּוֹ בַשָּׁלוֹם.

The Eternal One, enthroned above the flood, the Eternal One reigns for ever. You give strength to Your people, O God; You bless Your people with peace.

◆ ◆

לכה דודי

לְכָה דוֹדִי לִקְרַאת כַּלָּה, פְּנֵי שַׁבָּת נְקַבְּלָה.
לְכָה דוֹדִי לִקְרַאת כַּלָּה, פְּנֵי שַׁבָּת נְקַבְּלָה.

L'chah do-di lik-rat ka-lah, p'nei Shabbat n'ka-b'lah.

Beloved, come to meet the bride; beloved, come to greet Shabbat.

"שָׁמוֹר" וְ"זָכוֹר" בְּדִבּוּר אֶחָד, הִשְׁמִיעָנוּ אֵל הַמְיֻחָד.
יְיָ אֶחָד, וּשְׁמוֹ אֶחָד, לְשֵׁם וּלְתִפְאֶרֶת וְלִתְהִלָּה. לכה...

Keep and Remember: a single command, the Only God caused us
to hear; the Eternal is One, God's name is One, for honor and glory
and praise.
Beloved, come to meet the bride; beloved, come to greet Shabbat.

לִקְרַאת שַׁבָּת לְכוּ וְנֵלְכָה, כִּי הִיא מְקוֹר הַבְּרָכָה.
מֵרֹאשׁ מִקֶּדֶם נְסוּכָה, סוֹף מַעֲשֶׂה, בְּמַחֲשָׁבָה תְּחִלָּה. לכה...

Come with me to meet Shabbat, forever a fountain of blessing.
Still it flows, as from the start: the last of days, for which the first
was made.
Beloved, come to meet the bride; beloved, come to greet Shabbat.

הִתְעוֹרְרִי, הִתְעוֹרְרִי, כִּי בָא אוֹרֵךְ! קוּמִי אוֹרִי,
עוּרִי עוּרִי, שִׁיר דַּבֵּרִי; כְּבוֹד יְיָ עָלַיִךְ נִגְלָה. לכה...

Awake, awake, your light has come! Arise, shine, awake and sing;
the Eternal's glory dawns upon you.
Beloved, come to meet the bride; beloved, come to greet Shabbat.

בּוֹאִי בְשָׁלוֹם, עֲטֶרֶת בַּעְלָהּ, גַּם בְּשִׂמְחָה וּבְצָהֳלָה,
תּוֹךְ אֱמוּנֵי עַם סְגֻלָּה, בּוֹאִי כַלָּה! בּוֹאִי כַלָּה! לכה...

Enter in peace, O crown of your husband; enter in gladness, enter
in joy. Come to the people that keeps its faith. Enter, O bride!
Enter, O bride!
Beloved, come to meet the bride; beloved, come to greet Shabbat.

❖ ❖

Psalm 92

A SONG FOR THE SABBATH DAY   מִזְמוֹר שִׁיר לְיוֹם הַשַּׁבָּת

טוֹב לְהֹדוֹת לַיהוָה, וּלְזַמֵּר לְשִׁמְךָ עֶלְיוֹן,

לְהַגִּיד בַּבְּקֶר חַסְדֶּךָ, וֶאֱמוּנָתְךָ בַּלֵּילוֹת,

עֲלֵי־עָשׂוֹר וַעֲלֵי־נָבֶל, עֲלֵי הִגָּיוֹן בְּכִנּוֹר.

It is good to give thanks to the Eternal One,
to sing hymns to Your name, O Most High!
To tell of Your love in the morning,
Your faithfulness in the night;
to pluck the strings, to sound the lute,
to make the harp vibrate.

כִּי שִׂמַּחְתַּנִי, יְהוָה, בְּפָעֳלֶךָ, בְּמַעֲשֵׂי יָדֶיךָ אֲרַנֵּן.

מַה־גָּדְלוּ מַעֲשֶׂיךָ, יְהוָה! מְאֹד עָמְקוּ מַחְשְׁבֹתֶיךָ.

Your deeds, O God, fill me with gladness,
Your work moves me to song.
How great are Your works, O God!
How profound Your design!

אִישׁ־בַּעַר לֹא יֵדָע, וּכְסִיל לֹא־יָבִין אֶת־זֹאת:

בִּפְרֹחַ רְשָׁעִים כְּמוֹ־עֵשֶׂב, וַיָּצִיצוּ כָּל־פֹּעֲלֵי אָוֶן,

לְהִשָּׁמְדָם עֲדֵי־עַד. וְאַתָּה מָרוֹם לְעֹלָם, יְהוָה.

The fool will never learn,
the dullard never grasp this:
the wicked may flourish like grass,
all who do evil may blossom,
yet they are doomed to destruction,
while You, O God, are exalted for all time.

כִּי הִנֵּה אֹיְבֶיךָ, יְהוָה, כִּי־הִנֵּה אֹיְבֶיךָ יֹאבֵדוּ,

יִתְפָּרְדוּ כָּל־פֹּעֲלֵי אָוֶן. וַתָּרֶם כִּרְאֵים קַרְנִי, בַּלֹּתִי בְּשֶׁמֶן רַעֲנָן.

וַתַּבֵּט עֵינִי בְּשׁוּרָי, בַּקָּמִים עָלַי מְרֵעִים, תִּשְׁמַעְנָה אָזְנָי.

See how Your enemies, Eternal One,
see how Your enemies shall perish,
how all who do evil shall be scattered.

10

You lift up my head in pride,
I am bathed in freshening oil.
I shall see the defeat of my foes,
my ears shall hear of their fall.

צַדִּיק כַּתָּמָר יִפְרָח, כְּאֶרֶז בַּלְּבָנוֹן יִשְׂגֶּה.
שְׁתוּלִים בְּבֵית יְהֹוָה, בְּחַצְרוֹת אֱלֹהֵינוּ יַפְרִיחוּ.
עוֹד יְנוּבוּן בְּשֵׂיבָה, דְּשֵׁנִים וְרַעֲנַנִּים יִהְיוּ,
לְהַגִּיד כִּי־יָשָׁר יְהֹוָה, צוּרִי, וְלֹא־עַוְלָתָה בּוֹ.

The righteous shall flourish like palms,
grow tall like cedars in Lebanon.
Rooted in the house of their God,
they shall be ever fresh and green,
proclaiming that God is just,
my Rock, in whom there is no wrong.

Psalm 93

יְהֹוָה מָלָךְ, גֵּאוּת לָבֵשׁ; לָבֵשׁ יְהֹוָה, עֹז הִתְאַזָּר;
אַף־תִּכּוֹן תֵּבֵל, בַּל־תִּמּוֹט. נָכוֹן כִּסְאֲךָ מֵאָז, מֵעוֹלָם אָתָּה.
נָשְׂאוּ נְהָרוֹת, יְהֹוָה, נָשְׂאוּ נְהָרוֹת קוֹלָם, יִשְׂאוּ נְהָרוֹת דָּכְיָם;
מִקֹּלוֹת מַיִם רַבִּים, אַדִּירִים מִשְׁבְּרֵי־יָם, אַדִּיר בַּמָּרוֹם יְהֹוָה.
עֵדֹתֶיךָ נֶאֶמְנוּ מְאֹד; לְבֵיתְךָ נַאֲוָה־קֹדֶשׁ, יְהֹוָה, לְאֹרֶךְ יָמִים.

The Eternal One is enthroned, robed in grandeur;
The Eternal One is robed, girded with strength —
the One who founded the solid earth to be unmoving.

Ageless is Your throne, endless Your being.

The oceans cry out, Eternal God,
the oceans cry out their thunder,
the oceans rage in their fury;
but greater than the thunder of the torrents,
mightier than the breakers of the sea,
is the majesty of God on high!

Your law stands firm;
and in Your temple, O Eternal God,
holiness abides to the end of time!

11

All rise

READER'S KADDISH   חֲצִי קַדִּישׁ

יִתְגַּדַּל וְיִתְקַדַּשׁ שְׁמֵהּ רַבָּא בְּעָלְמָא דִּי־בְרָא כִרְעוּתֵהּ,
וְיַמְלִיךְ מַלְכוּתֵהּ בְּחַיֵּיכוֹן וּבְיוֹמֵיכוֹן וּבְחַיֵּי דְכָל־בֵּית
יִשְׂרָאֵל, בַּעֲגָלָא וּבִזְמַן קָרִיב, וְאִמְרוּ: אָמֵן.

יְהֵא שְׁמֵהּ רַבָּא מְבָרַךְ לְעָלַם וּלְעָלְמֵי עָלְמַיָּא.

יִתְבָּרַךְ וְיִשְׁתַּבַּח וְיִתְפָּאַר וְיִתְרוֹמַם וְיִתְנַשֵּׂא, וְיִתְהַדָּר
וְיִתְעַלֶּה וְיִתְהַלָּל שְׁמֵהּ דְּקוּדְשָׁא, בְּרִיךְ הוּא,
לְעֵלָּא מִן־כָּל־בִּרְכָתָא וְשִׁירָתָא, תֻּשְׁבְּחָתָא וְנֶחֱמָתָא
דַּאֲמִירָן בְּעָלְמָא, וְאִמְרוּ: אָמֵן.

Yit-ga-dal v'yit-ka-dash sh'mei ra-ba b'al-ma di-v'ra chir-u-tei,
v'yam-lich mal-chu-tei b'cha-yei-chon u-v'yo-mei-chon u-v'cha-yei
d'chol beit Yis-ra-eil, ba-a-ga-la u-viz-man ka-riv, v'im'ru: A-mein.

Y'hei sh'mei ra-ba m'va-rach l'a-lam u-l'al-mei al-ma-ya.

Yit-ba-rach v'yish-ta-bach v'yit-pa-ar, v'yit-ro-mam, v'yit-na-sei,
v'yit-ha-dar, v'yit-a-leh, v'yit-ha-lal sh'mei d'kud'sha, b'rich hu,

L'ei-la min kol bir-cha-ta v'shi-ra-ta, tush-b'cha-ta v'neh-cheh-ma-ta
da-a-mi-ran b'al-ma, v'im'ru: A-mein.

Let the glory of God be extolled, let God's great name be hallowed in the
world whose creation God willed. May God's reign begin in our own day,
our own lives, and the life of all Israel, and let us say: Amen.

Let God's great name be praised for ever and ever.

Let the name of the Holy One, the Blessed One, be glorified, exalted, and
honored, though God is beyond all the praises, songs, and adorations that
we can utter, and let us say: Amen.

The Sh'ma and Its Blessings   שמע וברכותיה

בָּרְכוּ אֶת־יְיָ הַמְבֹרָךְ!

Praise the One to whom praise is due!

בָּרוּךְ יְיָ הַמְבֹרָךְ לְעוֹלָם וָעֶד!

Praised be the One to whom praise is due, now and for ever!

CREATION   מעריב ערבים

בָּרוּךְ אַתָּה יְיָ, אֱלֹהֵינוּ מֶלֶךְ הָעוֹלָם,
אֲשֶׁר בִּדְבָרוֹ מַעֲרִיב עֲרָבִים, בְּחָכְמָה פּוֹתֵחַ שְׁעָרִים,
וּבִתְבוּנָה מְשַׁנֶּה עִתִּים, וּמַחֲלִיף אֶת־הַזְּמַנִּים,
וּמְסַדֵּר אֶת־הַכּוֹכָבִים בְּמִשְׁמְרוֹתֵיהֶם בָּרָקִיעַ כִּרְצוֹנוֹ.
בּוֹרֵא יוֹם וָלַיְלָה, גּוֹלֵל אוֹר מִפְּנֵי חֹשֶׁךְ וְחֹשֶׁךְ מִפְּנֵי אוֹר,
וּמַעֲבִיר יוֹם וּמֵבִיא לָיְלָה, וּמַבְדִּיל בֵּין יוֹם וּבֵין לָיְלָה,
יְיָ צְבָאוֹת שְׁמוֹ.
אֵל חַי וְקַיָּם, תָּמִיד יִמְלוֹךְ עָלֵינוּ לְעוֹלָם וָעֶד!
בָּרוּךְ אַתָּה יְיָ, הַמַּעֲרִיב עֲרָבִים.

Praised be our Eternal God, Ruler of the universe, whose word
brings on the evening, whose wisdom opens heaven's gates, whose
understanding makes the ages pass and the seasons alternate, and
whose will controls the stars as they travel through the skies.

You are Creator of day and night, rolling light away from
darkness, and darkness from light; You cause day to pass
and bring on the night; separating day from night; You
command the hosts of heaven!

May the living and eternal God rule us always, to the end
of time! We praise You, Eternal One, whose word makes
evening fall.

REVELATION אהבת עולם

אַהֲבַת עוֹלָם בֵּית יִשְׂרָאֵל עַמְּךָ אָהָבְתָּ.

תּוֹרָה וּמִצְוֹת, חֻקִּים וּמִשְׁפָּטִים אוֹתָנוּ לִמַּדְתָּ.

עַל־כֵּן, יְיָ אֱלֹהֵינוּ, בְּשָׁכְבֵּנוּ וּבְקוּמֵנוּ נָשִׂיחַ בְּחֻקֶּיךָ,

וְנִשְׂמַח בְּדִבְרֵי תוֹרָתֶךָ וּבְמִצְוֹתֶיךָ לְעוֹלָם וָעֶד.

כִּי הֵם חַיֵּינוּ וְאוֹרֶךְ יָמֵינוּ, וּבָהֶם נֶהְגֶּה יוֹמָם וָלָיְלָה.

וְאַהֲבָתְךָ אַל־תָּסוּר מִמֶּנוּ לְעוֹלָמִים!

בָּרוּךְ אַתָּה יְיָ, אוֹהֵב עַמּוֹ יִשְׂרָאֵל.

Unending is Your love for Your people, the House of Israel: Torah and Mitzvot, laws and precepts have You taught us.

Therefore, O God, when we lie down and when we rise up, we will meditate on Your laws and rejoice in Your Torah and Mitzvot for ever.

Day and night we will reflect on them, for they are our life and the length of our days. Then Your love shall never depart from our hearts! We praise You, Eternal One, who love Your people Israel.

◆ ◆

שְׁמַע יִשְׂרָאֵל יְהוָה אֱלֹהֵינוּ יְהוָה אֶחָד!
Sh'ma Yisrael: Adonai Eloheinu, Adonai Echad!

Hear, O Israel: the Eternal One is our God,
the Eternal God alone!

בָּרוּךְ שֵׁם כְּבוֹד מַלְכוּתוֹ לְעוֹלָם וָעֶד!
Baruch shem k'vod malchutoh l'olam va-ed!

Blessed is God's glorious majesty for ever and ever!

All are seated

14

וְאָהַבְתָּ אֵת יְהֹוָה אֱלֹהֶיךָ בְּכָל־לְבָבְךָ וּבְכָל־נַפְשְׁךָ וּבְכָל־מְאֹדֶךָ:
וְהָיוּ הַדְּבָרִים הָאֵלֶּה אֲשֶׁר אָנֹכִי מְצַוְּךָ הַיּוֹם עַל־לְבָבֶךָ:
וְשִׁנַּנְתָּם לְבָנֶיךָ וְדִבַּרְתָּ בָּם בְּשִׁבְתְּךָ בְּבֵיתֶךָ וּבְלֶכְתְּךָ בַדֶּרֶךְ
וּבְשָׁכְבְּךָ וּבְקוּמֶךָ: וּקְשַׁרְתָּם לְאוֹת עַל־יָדֶךָ וְהָיוּ לְטֹטָפֹת בֵּין
עֵינֶיךָ: וּכְתַבְתָּם עַל־מְזוּזֹת בֵּיתֶךָ וּבִשְׁעָרֶיךָ:

V'a-hav-ta et Adonai eh-lo-heh-cha b'chol l'va-v'cha u-v'chol naf-sh'cha u-v'chol m'o-deh-cha. V'ha-yu ha-d'va-rim ha-ei-leh a-sher a-no-chi m'tza-v'cha ha-yom al l'va-veh-cha. V'shi-nan-tam l'va-neh-cha v'di-bar-ta bam b'shiv-t'cha b'vei-teh-cha u-v'lech-t'cha va-deh-rech u-v'shoch-b'cha u-v'ku-meh-cha. U-k'shar-tam l'oht al ya-deh-cha v'ha-yu l'toh-ta-foht bein ei-neh-cha; u-ch'tav-tam al m'zu-zoht bei-teh-cha u-vi-sh'a-reh-cha.

You shall love the Eternal One, your God, with all your heart, with all your mind, with all your being. Set these words, which I command you this day, upon your heart. Teach them faithfully to your children; speak of them in your home and on your way, when you lie down and when you rise up. Bind them as a sign upon your hand; let them be a symbol before your eyes; inscribe them on the doorposts of your house, and on your gates.

לְמַעַן תִּזְכְּרוּ וַעֲשִׂיתֶם אֶת־כָּל־מִצְוֹתָי וִהְיִיתֶם קְדֹשִׁים
לֵאלֹהֵיכֶם: אֲנִי יְהֹוָה אֱלֹהֵיכֶם אֲשֶׁר הוֹצֵאתִי אֶתְכֶם
מֵאֶרֶץ מִצְרַיִם לִהְיוֹת לָכֶם לֵאלֹהִים. אֲנִי יְהֹוָה אֱלֹהֵיכֶם:

L'ma-an tiz-k'ru va-a-si-tem et kol mitz-vo-tai, vi-h'yi-tem k'doh-shim lei-lo-hei-chem. Ani Adonai eh-lo-hei-chem a-sher ho-tzei-ti et-chem mei-eh-retz mitz-ra-yim li-h'yoht la-chem lei-lo-him. Ani Ado-nai eh-lo-hei-chem.

Be mindful of all My Mitzvot, and do them: so shall you consecrate yourselves to your God. I am your Eternal God who led you out of Egypt to be your God; I am your Eternal God.

גְאוּלָה

אֱמֶת וֶאֱמוּנָה כָּל־זֹאת, וְקַיָּם עָלֵינוּ כִּי הוּא יְיָ אֱלֹהֵינוּ וְאֵין
זוּלָתוֹ, וַאֲנַחְנוּ יִשְׂרָאֵל עַמּוֹ.

הַפּוֹדֵנוּ מִיַּד מְלָכִים, מַלְכֵּנוּ הַגּוֹאֲלֵנוּ מִכַּף כָּל־הֶעָרִיצִים.

הָעֹשֶׂה גְדֹלוֹת עַד אֵין חֵקֶר, וְנִפְלָאוֹת עַד־אֵין מִסְפָּר.

הַשָּׂם נַפְשֵׁנוּ בַּחַיִּים, וְלֹא־נָתַן לַמּוֹט רַגְלֵנוּ.

הָעֹשֶׂה לָּנוּ נִסִּים בְּפַרְעֹה, אוֹתוֹת וּמוֹפְתִים בְּאַדְמַת בְּנֵי חָם.

וַיּוֹצֵא אֶת־עַמּוֹ יִשְׂרָאֵל מִתּוֹכָם לְחֵרוּת עוֹלָם.

וְרָאוּ בָנָיו וּבְנוֹתָיו גְּבוּרָתוֹ; שִׁבְּחוּ וְהוֹדוּ לִשְׁמוֹ. וּמַלְכוּתוֹ
בְּרָצוֹן קִבְּלוּ עֲלֵיהֶם. מֹשֶׁה וּמִרְיָם וּבְנֵי יִשְׂרָאֵל לְךָ עָנוּ
שִׁירָה בְּשִׂמְחָה רַבָּה, וְאָמְרוּ כֻלָּם:

All this we hold to be true and sure; You alone are our God;
there is none else, and we are Israel Your people.

You are our Ruler: You deliver us from the hand of
oppressors, and save us from the fist of tyrants,

You do wonders without number,
marvels that pass our understanding.

You give us our life; by Your help we survive
all who seek our destruction.

You did wonders for us in the land of Egypt,
miracles and marvels in the land of Pharaoh,

You led Your people Israel out,
forever to serve You in freedom.

When Your children witnessed Your power, they extolled You and
gave You thanks; willingly they enthroned You; and, full of joy,
Moses, Miriam, and all Israel sang this song:

מִי־כָמְכָה בָּאֵלִם, יְהֹוָה? מִי כָּמְכָה, נֶאְדָּר בַּקֹּדֶשׁ,
נוֹרָא תְהִלֹּת, עֹשֵׂה פֶלֶא?
מַלְכוּתְךָ רָאוּ בָנֶיךָ, בּוֹקֵעַ יָם לִפְנֵי מֹשֶׁה; זֶה אֵלִי!
עָנוּ וְאָמְרוּ: יְהֹוָה יִמְלֹךְ לְעֹלָם וָעֶד!
וְנֶאֱמַר: כִּי פָדָה יְיָ אֶת־יַעֲקֹב, וּגְאָלוֹ מִיַּד חָזָק
מִמֶּנּוּ. בָּרוּךְ אַתָּה יְיָ, גָּאַל יִשְׂרָאֵל.

Mi cha-mo-cha ba-ei-lim, Adonai? Mi ka-mo-cha, ne-dar ba-ko-
desh, no-ra t'hi-loht, o-sei feh-leh?
Mal-chu-t'cha ra-u va-neh-cha, bo-kei-a yam lif-nei Mo-sheh; zeh
ei-li! a-nu v'am-ru: Adonai yim-loch l'o-lam va-ed.
V'neh-eh-mar: Ki fa-da Adonai et Ya-a-kov, u-g'a-lo mi-yad cha-zak
mi-meh-nu. Ba-ruch a-ta Adonai, ga-al Yis-ra-el.

Who is like You, Eternal One, among the gods that are worshipped?
Who is like You, majestic in holiness, awesome in splendor, doing
wonders?

In their escape from the sea, Your children saw Your sovereign might
displayed. This is my God! they cried. The Eternal One will reign for
ever and ever

And it has been said: The Eternal One delivered Jacob, and redeemed
us from the hand of one stronger than ourselves. We praise You,
Eternal One, Redeemer of Israel.

DIVINE PROVIDENCE   הַשְׁכִּיבֵנוּ

הַשְׁכִּיבֵנוּ, יְיָ אֱלֹהֵינוּ, לְשָׁלוֹם, וְהַעֲמִידֵנוּ, מַלְכֵּנוּ, לְחַיִּים.
וּפְרוֹשׁ עָלֵינוּ סֻכַּת שְׁלוֹמֶךָ, וְתַקְּנֵנוּ בְּעֵצָה טוֹבָה מִלְּפָנֶיךָ,
וְהוֹשִׁיעֵנוּ לְמַעַן שְׁמֶךָ, וְהָגֵן בַּעֲדֵנוּ. וְהָסֵר מֵעָלֵינוּ אוֹיֵב דֶּבֶר
וְחֶרֶב וְרָעָב וְיָגוֹן; וְהָסֵר שָׂטָן מִלְּפָנֵינוּ וּמֵאַחֲרֵינוּ, וּבְצֵל
כְּנָפֶיךָ תַּסְתִּירֵנוּ, כִּי אֵל שׁוֹמְרֵנוּ וּמַצִּילֵנוּ אָתָּה, כִּי אֵל מֶלֶךְ
חַנּוּן וְרַחוּם אָתָּה. וּשְׁמוֹר צֵאתֵנוּ וּבוֹאֵנוּ לְחַיִּים וּלְשָׁלוֹם
מֵעַתָּה וְעַד עוֹלָם. בָּרוּךְ אַתָּה יְיָ, הַפּוֹרֵשׂ סֻכַּת שָׁלוֹם עָלֵינוּ,
וְעַל־כָּל־עַמּוֹ־יִשְׂרָאֵל, וְעַל יְרוּשָׁלָיִם.

Grant that we may lie down in peace, Eternal God, and raise us up, O Sovereign, to life renewed. Spread over us the shelter of Your peace; guide us with Your good counsel; and for Your name's sake, be our Help.

Shield us from hatred and plague; keep us from war and famine and anguish; subdue our inclination to evil. O God, our Guardian and Helper, our gracious and merciful Ruler, give us refuge in the shadow of Your wings. O guard our coming and our going, that now and always we have life and peace.

We praise You, Eternal One, whose shelter of peace is spread over us, over all Your people Israel, and over Jerusalem.

THE COVENANT OF SHABBAT   ושמרו

וְשָׁמְרוּ בְנֵי־יִשְׂרָאֵל אֶת־הַשַּׁבָּת, לַעֲשׂוֹת אֶת־הַשַּׁבָּת לְדֹרֹתָם
בְּרִית עוֹלָם. בֵּינִי וּבֵין בְּנֵי יִשְׂרָאֵל אוֹת הִיא לְעֹלָם, כִּי־שֵׁשֶׁת
יָמִים עָשָׂה יְהוָה אֶת־הַשָּׁמַיִם וְאֶת־הָאָרֶץ, וּבַיּוֹם הַשְּׁבִיעִי
שָׁבַת וַיִּנָּפַשׁ.

V'sham'ru v'nei Yis-ra-el et ha-sha-bat, la-a-soht et ha-sha-bat l'doh-ro-tam, b'rit o-lam. Bei-ni u-vein b'nei Yis-ra-el ot hi l'o-lam, ki shei-shet ya-mim a-sa A-do-nai et ha-sha-ma-yim v'et ha-a-rets, u-va-yom ha-sh'vi-i sha-vat va-yi-na-fash.

The people of Israel shall keep the Sabbath, observing the Sabbath in every generation as a covenant for all time. It is a sign for ever between Me and the people of Israel, for in six days the Eternal God made heaven and earth, taking rest and refreshment on the seventh day.

All rise

T'filah תפלה

אֲדֹנָי שְׂפָתַי תִּפְתָּח וּפִי יַגִּיד תְּהִלָּתֶךָ:

Eternal God, open my lips, that my mouth may declare Your glory.

GOD OF ALL GENERATIONS אבות ואמהות

בָּרוּךְ אַתָּה יְיָ, אֱלֹהֵינוּ וֵאלֹהֵי אֲבוֹתֵינוּ וְאִמּוֹתֵינוּ:

אֱלֹהֵי אַבְרָהָם, אֱלֹהֵי יִצְחָק, וֵאלֹהֵי יַעֲקֹב.

אֱלֹהֵי שָׂרָה, אֱלֹהֵי רִבְקָה, אֱלֹהֵי לֵאָה, וֵאלֹהֵי רָחֵל.

הָאֵל הַגָּדוֹל הַגִּבּוֹר וְהַנּוֹרָא, אֵל עֶלְיוֹן,

גּוֹמֵל חֲסָדִים טוֹבִים וְקוֹנֵה הַכֹּל,

וְזוֹכֵר חַסְדֵי אָבוֹת וְאִמָּהוֹת,

וּמֵבִיא גְאֻלָּה לִבְנֵי בְנֵיהֶם, לְמַעַן שְׁמוֹ בְּאַהֲבָה.

ON SHABBAT SHUVAH ADD:

זָכְרֵנוּ לְחַיִּים, מֶלֶךְ חָפֵץ בַּחַיִּים,
וְכָתְבֵנוּ בְּסֵפֶר הַחַיִּים, לְמַעַנְךָ אֱלֹהִים חַיִּים.

מֶלֶךְ עוֹזֵר וּמוֹשִׁיעַ וּמָגֵן.

בָּרוּךְ אַתָּה יְיָ, מָגֵן אַבְרָהָם וְעֶזְרַת שָׂרָה.

Ba-ruch a-ta Adonai, Eh-lo-hei-nu vei-lo-hei a-vo-tei-nu v'i-mo-
tei-nu:
Eh-lo-hei Av-ra-ham, eh-lo-hei Yitz-chak, vei-lo-hei Ya-a-kov.
Eh-lo-hei Sa-rah, eh-lo-hei Riv-kah, eh-lo-hei Lei-ah, vei-lo-hei
Ra-cheil.
Ha-eil ha-ga-dol ha-gi-bor v'ha-no-ra, eil el-yon. Go-meil cha-sa-dim
toh-vim, v'ko-nei ha-kol, v'zo-cheir chas-dei a-voht v'i-ma-hoht,
u-mei-vi g'u-la li-v'nei v'nei-hem, l'ma-an sh'mo, b'a-ha-vah.
Meh-lech o-zeir u-mo-shi-a u-ma-gein.
Ba-ruch a-ta Adonai, ma-gein Av-ra-ham v'ez-rat Sa-rah.

Praised be our God, the God of our fathers and our mothers: God of Abraham, God of Isaac, and God of Jacob; God of Sarah, God of Rebekah, God of Leah and God of Rachel; great, mighty, and awesome God, God supreme.

Ruler of all the living, Your ways are ways of love. You remember the faithfulness of our ancestors, and in love bring redemption to their children's children for the sake of Your name.

ON SHABBAT SHUVAH ADD:

Remember us unto life, Sovereign who delights in life, and inscribe us in the Book of Life, that Your will may prevail, O God of life.

You are our Sovereign and our Help, our Redeemer and our Shield. We praise You, Eternal One, Shield of Abraham, Protector of Sarah.

GOD'S POWER   גבורות

אַתָּה גִבּוֹר לְעוֹלָם, אֲדֹנָי, מְחַיֵּה הַכֹּל אַתָּה, רַב לְהוֹשִׁיעַ.

מְכַלְכֵּל חַיִּים בְּחֶסֶד, מְחַיֵּה הַכֹּל בְּרַחֲמִים רַבִּים.

סוֹמֵךְ נוֹפְלִים, וְרוֹפֵא חוֹלִים, וּמַתִּיר אֲסוּרִים, וּמְקַיֵּם אֱמוּנָתוֹ

לִישֵׁנֵי עָפָר. מִי כָמוֹךָ בַּעַל גְּבוּרוֹת, וּמִי דוֹמֶה לָּךְ,

מֶלֶךְ מֵמִית וּמְחַיֵּה וּמַצְמִיחַ יְשׁוּעָה?

ON SHABBAT SHUVAH ADD:

מִי כָמוֹךָ, אַב הָרַחֲמִים,

זוֹכֵר יְצוּרָיו לְחַיִּים בְּרַחֲמִים?

וְנֶאֱמָן אַתָּה לְהַחֲיוֹת הַכֹּל. בָּרוּךְ אַתָּה יְיָ, מְחַיֵּה הַכֹּל.

A-ta gi-bor l'o-lam, Adonai, m'cha-yei ha-kol a-ta, rav l'ho-shi-a. M'chal-keil cha-yim b'cheh-sed, m'cha-yei ha-kol b'ra-cha-mim ra-bim. So-meich no-f'lim, v'ro-fei cho-lim, u-ma-tir a-su-rim, u-m'ka-yeim eh-mu-na-toh li-shei-nei a-far. Mi cha-mo-cha ba-al g'vu-roht, u-mi doh-meh lach, meh-lech mei-mit u-m'cha-yeh u-matz-mi-ach y'shu-a?

V'neh-eh-man a-ta l'ha-cha-yoht ha-kol, Ba-ruch a-ta Adonai, m'cha-yei ha-kol.

Eternal is Your might, O God; all life is Your gift; great is Your power to save!

With love You sustain the living, with great compassion give life to all. You send help to the falling and healing to the sick; You bring freedom to the captive and keep faith with those who sleep in the dust.

Who is like You, Mighty One? Who is Your equal, Author of life and death, Source of salvation?

ON SHABBAT SHUVAH ADD:

Who is like You, Source of mercy?

In compassion You sustain the life of Your children.

We praise You, Eternal God, the Source of life.

THE HOLINESS OF GOD   קְדוּשַׁת הַשֵּׁם

אַתָּה קָדוֹשׁ וְשִׁמְךָ קָדוֹשׁ, וּקְדוֹשִׁים בְּכָל־יוֹם יְהַלְלוּךָ סֶּלָה.

* בָּרוּךְ אַתָּה יְיָ, הָאֵל הַקָּדוֹשׁ.

*ON SHABBAT SHUVAH CONCLUDE:

בָּרוּךְ אַתָּה יְיָ, הַמֶּלֶךְ הַקָּדוֹשׁ.

You are holy, Your name is holy, and those who strive to be holy declare Your glory day by day.

*We praise You, Eternal One, the holy God.

*ON SHABBAT SHUVAH CONCLUDE:

We praise You, Eternal One: You rule in holiness.

All are seated

21

THE HOLINESS OF SHABBAT   קְדוּשַׁת הַיּוֹם

אַתָּה קִדַּשְׁתָּ אֶת־יוֹם הַשְּׁבִיעִי לִשְׁמֶךָ;
תַּכְלִית מַעֲשֵׂה שָׁמַיִם וָאָרֶץ, וּבֵרַכְתּוֹ מִכָּל הַיָּמִים
וְקִדַּשְׁתּוֹ מִכָּל־הַזְּמַנִּים, וְכֵן כָּתוּב בְּתוֹרָתֶךָ:

You set the seventh day apart for Your service; it is the goal of
creation, more blessed than other days, more sacred than other
times, as we read in the story of creation:

וַיְכֻלּוּ הַשָּׁמַיִם וְהָאָרֶץ וְכָל־צְבָאָם: וַיְכַל אֱלֹהִים בַּיּוֹם
הַשְּׁבִיעִי מְלַאכְתּוֹ אֲשֶׁר עָשָׂה. וַיִּשְׁבֹּת בַּיּוֹם הַשְּׁבִיעִי מִכָּל־
מְלַאכְתּוֹ אֲשֶׁר עָשָׂה: וַיְבָרֶךְ אֱלֹהִים אֶת־יוֹם הַשְּׁבִיעִי וַיְקַדֵּשׁ
אֹתוֹ, כִּי בוֹ שָׁבַת מִכָּל־מְלַאכְתּוֹ אֲשֶׁר־בָּרָא אֱלֹהִים לַעֲשׂוֹת:

Now the whole universe—sky, earth, and all their array—was
completed. With the seventh day God ended the work of creation,
resting on the seventh day, with all the work completed. Then God
blessed the seventh day and sanctified it, this day having
completed the work of creation.

אֱלֹהֵינוּ וֵאלֹהֵי אֲבוֹתֵינוּ וְאִמּוֹתֵינוּ, רְצֵה בִמְנוּחָתֵנוּ.
קַדְּשֵׁנוּ בְּמִצְוֹתֶיךָ וְתֵן חֶלְקֵנוּ בְּתוֹרָתֶךָ. שַׂבְּעֵנוּ מִטּוּבֶךָ,
וְשַׂמְּחֵנוּ בִּישׁוּעָתֶךָ, וְטַהֵר לִבֵּנוּ לְעָבְדְּךָ בֶּאֱמֶת.
וְהַנְחִילֵנוּ, יְיָ אֱלֹהֵינוּ, בְּאַהֲבָה וּבְרָצוֹן שַׁבַּת קָדְשֶׁךָ,
וְיָנוּחוּ בָהּ יִשְׂרָאֵל מְקַדְּשֵׁי שְׁמֶךָ.
בָּרוּךְ אַתָּה יְיָ, מְקַדֵּשׁ הַשַּׁבָּת.

*Our God, God of our fathers and our mothers, may our rest
on this day be pleasing in Your sight. Sanctify us with Your
Mitzvot, and let Your Torah be our way of life. Satisfy us
with Your goodness, gladden us with Your salvation, and
purify our hearts to serve You in truth. In Your gracious love,
Eternal God, let Your holy Sabbath remain our heritage,
that all Israel, hallowing Your name, may find rest and
peace. We praise You, Eternal One, for the Sabbath and its
holiness.*

WORSHIP עבודה

רְצֵה, יְיָ אֱלֹהֵינוּ, בְּעַמְּךָ יִשְׂרָאֵל, וּתְפִלָּתָם בְּאַהֲבָה תְקַבֵּל,
וּתְהִי לְרָצוֹן תָּמִיד עֲבוֹדַת יִשְׂרָאֵל עַמֶּךָ.
אֵל קָרוֹב לְכָל־קֹרְאָיו, פְּנֵה אֶל עֲבָדֶיךָ וְחָנֵּנוּ;
שְׁפוֹךְ רוּחֲךָ עָלֵינוּ, וְתֶחֱזֶינָה עֵינֵינוּ בְּשׁוּבְךָ לְצִיּוֹן בְּרַחֲמִים.
בָּרוּךְ אַתָּה יְיָ, הַמַּחֲזִיר שְׁכִינָתוֹ לְצִיּוֹן.

Be gracious, Eternal God, to Your people Israel, and receive our
prayers with love. May our worship always be acceptable to You.

*Fill us with the knowledge that You are near to all who seek
You in truth. Let our eyes behold Your presence in our midst
and in the midst of our people in Zion. We praise You,
Eternal One, whose presence gives life to Zion and all Israel.*

ON ROSH CHODESH AND CHOL HA-MO-EID:

אֱלֹהֵינוּ וֵאלֹהֵי אֲבוֹתֵינוּ וְאִמּוֹתֵינוּ, יַעֲלֶה וְיָבֹא וְיִזָּכֵר זִכְרוֹנֵנוּ
וְזִכְרוֹן כָּל־עַמְּךָ בֵּית יִשְׂרָאֵל לְפָנֶיךָ לְטוֹבָה לְחֵן לְחֶסֶד
וּלְרַחֲמִים, לְחַיִּים וּלְשָׁלוֹם בְּיוֹם

• רֹאשׁ הַחֹדֶשׁ הַזֶּה.

• חַג הַמַּצוֹת הַזֶּה.

• חַג הַסֻּכּוֹת הַזֶּה.

זָכְרֵנוּ יְיָ אֱלֹהֵינוּ, בּוֹ לְטוֹבָה.   אָמֵן.

וּפָקְדֵנוּ בוֹ לִבְרָכָה.   אָמֵן.

וְהוֹשִׁיעֵנוּ בוֹ לְחַיִּים.   אָמֵן.

Our God , God of our fathers and our mothers, be mindful of Your
people Israel on this

• first day of the new month,

• day of Pesach,

• day of Sukkot,

and renew in us love and compassion, goodness, life, and peace.

23

This day remember us for well-being.   *Amen.*

This day bless us with Your nearness.   *Amen.*

This day help us to a fuller life.   *Amen.*

◆ ◆

THANKSGIVING   הוֹדָאָה

מוֹדִים אֲנַחְנוּ לָךְ, שָׁאַתָּה הוּא יְיָ אֱלֹהֵינוּ וֵאלֹהֵי אֲבוֹתֵינוּ
וְאִמּוֹתֵינוּ לְעוֹלָם וָעֶד. צוּר חַיֵּינוּ, מָגֵן יִשְׁעֵנוּ, אַתָּה הוּא
לְדוֹר וָדוֹר. נוֹדֶה לְךָ וּנְסַפֵּר תְּהִלָּתֶךָ, עַל־חַיֵּינוּ הַמְּסוּרִים
בְּיָדֶךָ, וְעַל־נִשְׁמוֹתֵינוּ הַפְּקוּדוֹת לָךְ, וְעַל־נִסֶּיךָ שֶׁבְּכָל־יוֹם
עִמָּנוּ, וְעַל־נִפְלְאוֹתֶיךָ וְטוֹבוֹתֶיךָ שֶׁבְּכָל־עֵת, עֶרֶב וָבֹקֶר
וְצָהֳרָיִם. הַטּוֹב: כִּי לֹא־כָלוּ רַחֲמֶיךָ, וְהַמְרַחֵם: כִּי־לֹא תַמּוּ
חֲסָדֶיךָ, מֵעוֹלָם קִוִּינוּ לָךְ. וְעַל כֻּלָּם יִתְבָּרַךְ וְיִתְרוֹמַם שִׁמְךָ,
מַלְכֵּנוּ, תָּמִיד לְעוֹלָם וָעֶד.

ON SHABBAT SHUVAH ADD:

וּכְתוֹב לְחַיִּים טוֹבִים כָּל־בְּנֵי בְרִיתֶךָ.

וְכֹל הַחַיִּים יוֹדוּךָ סֶּלָה, וִיהַלְלוּ אֶת שִׁמְךָ בֶּאֱמֶת, הָאֵל
יְשׁוּעָתֵנוּ וְעֶזְרָתֵנוּ סֶלָה. בָּרוּךְ אַתָּה יְיָ, הַטּוֹב שִׁמְךָ וּלְךָ נָאֶה
לְהוֹדוֹת.

*We gratefully acknowledge that You are our God and the
God of our people, the God of all the generations. You are
the Rock of our life, the Power that shields us in every age.
We thank You and sing Your praises: for our lives, which are
in Your hand; for our souls, which are in Your keeping; for
the signs of Your presence we encounter every day; and for
Your wondrous gifts at all times, morning, noon, and night.
You are Goodness: Your mercies never end; You are
Compassion: Your love will never fail. You have always been
our hope.*

For all these things, O Sovereign God, let Your name be for ever
exalted and blessed.

24

Shabbat Evening Service I

ON SHABBAT SHUVAH ADD:

Let life abundant be the heritage of all the children
of Your covenant.

O God our Redeemer and Helper, let all who live affirm You and
praise Your name in truth. Eternal God, whose nature is Goodness, we give You thanks and praise.

ON CHANUKAH ADD:

עַל הַנִּסִּים וְעַל הַפֻּרְקָן וְעַל הַגְּבוּרוֹת וְעַל הַתְּשׁוּעוֹת וְעַל
הַמִּלְחָמוֹת שֶׁעָשִׂיתָ לַאֲבוֹתֵינוּ וּלְאִמּוֹתֵינוּ בַּיָּמִים הָהֵם בַּזְּמַן
הַזֶּה. בִּימֵי מַתִּתְיָהוּ בֶּן־יוֹחָנָן כֹּהֵן גָּדוֹל, חַשְׁמוֹנַאי וּבָנָיו,
כְּשֶׁעָמְדָה מַלְכוּת יָוָן הָרְשָׁעָה עַל עַמְּךָ יִשְׂרָאֵל, לְהַשְׁכִּיחָם
תּוֹרָתֶךָ וּלְהַעֲבִירָם מֵחֻקֵּי רְצוֹנֶךָ. וְאַתָּה בְּרַחֲמֶיךָ הָרַבִּים
עָמַדְתָּ לָהֶם בְּעֵת צָרָתָם, רַבְתָּ אֶת־רִיבָם, דַּנְתָּ אֶת־דִּינָם,
נָקַמְתָּ אֶת־נִקְמָתָם, מָסַרְתָּ גִּבּוֹרִים בְּיַד חַלָּשִׁים, וְרַבִּים בְּיַד
מְעַטִּים, וּטְמֵאִים בְּיַד טְהוֹרִים, וּרְשָׁעִים בְּיַד צַדִּיקִים, וְזֵדִים
בְּיַד עוֹסְקֵי תוֹרָתֶךָ. וּלְךָ עָשִׂיתָ שֵׁם גָּדוֹל וְקָדוֹשׁ בְּעוֹלָמֶךָ,
וּלְעַמְּךָ יִשְׂרָאֵל עָשִׂיתָ תְּשׁוּעָה גְדוֹלָה וּפֻרְקָן כְּהַיּוֹם הַזֶּה,
וְאַחַר כֵּן בָּאוּ בָנֶיךָ לִדְבִיר בֵּיתֶךָ, וּפִנּוּ אֶת־הֵיכָלֶךָ, וְטִהֲרוּ
אֶת־מִקְדָּשֶׁךָ, וְהִדְלִיקוּ נֵרוֹת בְּחַצְרוֹת קָדְשֶׁךָ, וְקָבְעוּ שְׁמוֹנַת
יְמֵי חֲנֻכָּה אֵלוּ, לְהוֹדוֹת וּלְהַלֵּל לְשִׁמְךָ הַגָּדוֹל.

We give thanks for the redeeming wonders and the mighty deeds
by which at this season our people was saved in days of old.
In the days of the Hasmoneans, a tyrant rose up against our ancestors, determined to make them forget Your Torah, and to turn
them away from obedience to Your will. But You were at their
side in time of trouble. You gave them strength to struggle and to
triumph, that they might serve You in freedom.
Through the power of Your spirit the weak defeated the strong,
the few prevailed over the many, and the righteous were trium-
phant. Then Your children returned to Your house, to purify the
sanctuary and to kindle its lights. And they dedicated these days
to give thanks and praise to Your great name.

◆ ◆

25

PEACE   ברכת שלום

שָׁלוֹם רָב עַל־יִשְׂרָאֵל עַמְּךָ תָּשִׂים לְעוֹלָם,

כִּי אַתָּה הוּא מֶלֶךְ אָדוֹן לְכָל הַשָּׁלוֹם. וְטוֹב בְּעֵינֶיךָ

לְבָרֵךְ אֶת־עַמְּךָ יִשְׂרָאֵל בְּכָל־עֵת וּבְכָל־שָׁעָה בִּשְׁלוֹמֶךָ.

* בָּרוּךְ אַתָּה יְיָ, הַמְבָרֵךְ אֶת־עַמּוֹ יִשְׂרָאֵל בַּשָּׁלוֹם.

*ON SHABBAT SHUVAH CONCLUDE:

בְּסֵפֶר חַיִּים וּבְרָכָה נִכָּתֵב לְחַיִּים טוֹבִים וּלְשָׁלוֹם.
בָּרוּךְ אַתָּה יְיָ, עוֹשֵׂה הַשָּׁלוֹם.

*O Sovereign Source of peace, let Israel Your people know
enduring peace, for it is good in Your sight to bless Israel
continually with Your peace.*

*We praise You, Eternal One: You bless Israel with peace.

*ON SHABBAT SHUVAH CONCLUDE:

Inscribe us in the Book of life, blessing, and peace. We praise You,
Eternal One, the Source of peace.

SILENT PRAYER

אֱלֹהַי, נְצֹר לְשׁוֹנִי מֵרָע, וּשְׂפָתַי מִדַּבֵּר מִרְמָה. וְלִמְקַלְלַי נַפְשִׁי

תִדּוֹם וְנַפְשִׁי כֶּעָפָר לַכֹּל תִּהְיֶה. פְּתַח לִבִּי בְּתוֹרָתֶךָ, וּבְמִצְוֹתֶיךָ

תִּרְדּוֹף נַפְשִׁי. וְכָל־הַחוֹשְׁבִים עָלַי רָעָה, מְהֵרָה הָפֵר עֲצָתָם

וְקַלְקֵל מַחֲשַׁבְתָּם. עֲשֵׂה לְמַעַן שְׁמֶךָ, עֲשֵׂה לְמַעַן יְמִינֶךָ, עֲשֵׂה

לְמַעַן קְדֻשָּׁתֶךָ, עֲשֵׂה לְמַעַן תּוֹרָתֶךָ; לְמַעַן יֵחָלְצוּן יְדִידֶיךָ,

הוֹשִׁיעָה יְמִינְךָ וַעֲנֵנִי.

O God, keep my tongue from evil and my lips from deceit. Help
me to be silent in the face of derision, humble in the presence of
all. Open my heart to Your Torah, and I will hasten to do Your
Mitzvot. Save me with Your power; in time of trouble be my
answer, that those who love You may rejoice.

◆ ◆

יִהְיוּ לְרָצוֹן אִמְרֵי־פִי וְהֶגְיוֹן לִבִּי לְפָנֶיךָ, יְהֹוָה, צוּרִי וְגֹאֲלִי.

May the words of my mouth, and the meditations of my heart, be acceptable to You, O God, my Rock and my Redeemer.

◆

עֹשֶׂה שָׁלוֹם בִּמְרוֹמָיו, הוּא יַעֲשֶׂה שָׁלוֹם עָלֵינוּ
וְעַל־כָּל־יִשְׂרָאֵל, וְאִמְרוּ אָמֵן.

May the One who causes peace to reign in the high heavens let peace descend on us, on all Israel, and all the world.

27

(The following may be added if desired)

ESSENCE OF THE T'FILAH   מֵעֵין שֶׁבַע

בָּרוּךְ אַתָּה יְיָ, אֱלֹהֵינוּ וֵאלֹהֵי אֲבוֹתֵינוּ וְאִמּוֹתֵינוּ;
אֱלֹהֵי אַבְרָהָם, אֱלֹהֵי יִצְחָק, וֵאלֹהֵי יַעֲקֹב.
אֱלֹהֵי שָׂרָה, אֱלֹהֵי רִבְקָה, אֱלֹהֵי לֵאָה, וֵאלֹהֵי רָחֵל.
הָאֵל הַגָּדוֹל הַגִּבּוֹר וְהַנּוֹרָא, אֵל עֶלְיוֹן, קֹנֵה שָׁמַיִם וָאָרֶץ.

Praised be our God, the God of our fathers and our mothers: God
of Abraham, God of Isaac, and God of Jacob; God of Sarah, God
of Rebekah, God of Leah and God of Rachel; great, mighty, and
awesome God, God supreme, Maker of heaven and earth.

מָגֵן אָבוֹת בִּדְבָרוֹ, עֶזְרַת אִמָּהוֹת בְּפִקְדָתוֹ,
מְחַיֵּה הַכֹּל בְּמַאֲמָרוֹ.
הָאֵל הַקָּדוֹשׁ, שֶׁאֵין כָּמוֹהוּ, הַמֵּנִיחַ לְעַמּוֹ בְּיוֹם שַׁבַּת קָדְשׁוֹ.
כִּי בָם רָצָה לְהָנִיחַ לָהֶם. לְפָנָיו נַעֲבוֹד בְּיִרְאָה וָפַחַד,
וְנוֹדֶה לִשְׁמוֹ בְּכָל־יוֹם תָּמִיד מֵעֵין הַבְּרָכוֹת. אֵל הַהוֹדָאוֹת,
אֲדוֹן הַשָּׁלוֹם, מְקַדֵּשׁ הַשַּׁבָּת וּמְבָרֵךְ שְׁבִיעִי, וּמֵנִיחַ
בִּקְדָשָׁה לְעַם מְדֻשְּׁנֵי עֹנֶג, זֵכֶר לְמַעֲשֵׂה בְרֵאשִׁית.

Your word was a shield and protection to our ancestors, You are
the Source of all life. You are the holy God, beyond compare. You
give rest to Your people on Your holy Sabbath day. In awe and
trembling we will serve You, and day after day affirm You. Source
of peace, God to whom thanks are due, You hallow and bless the
Sabbath, in remembrance of the work of creation. In its rest our
people finds abounding joy.

The Service for the reading of Torah is on page 65

Aleinu is on page 73 or page 76

Shabbat Evening Service II

(For congregations where the lights are kindled in the synagogue)

הדלקת הנרות

As these candles give light to all who behold them, so may we give light to all who behold us.

As their brightness reminds us of the generations of Israel who have kindled light, so may we, in our own day, be among those who kindle light.

◆ ◆

בָּרוּךְ אַתָּה יְיָ, אֱלֹהֵינוּ מֶלֶךְ הָעוֹלָם, אֲשֶׁר קִדְּשָׁנוּ
בְּמִצְוֹתָיו וְצִוָּנוּ לְהַדְלִיק נֵר שֶׁל שַׁבָּת.

Ba-ruch a-ta Adonai, Eh-lo-hei-nu meh-lech ha-o-lam, ah-sher kid'sha-nu b'mitz-vo-tav, v'tzi-va-nu l'had-lik ner shel Shabbat.

Praised be our Eternal God, Ruler of the universe: You hallow us with Mitzvot, and command us to kindle the lights of Shabbat.

◆ ◆

Let there be joy!
Let there be light!

Let there be peace!
Let there be Shabbat!

29

A PRAYER

O Source of light and truth, Creator of the eternal law of goodness, and of the impulse within us for justice and mercy, we pray that this hour of worship may be one of vision and inspiration. Help us to find knowledge by which to live; lead us to take the words we shall speak into our hearts and our lives.

Bless all who enter this sanctuary in search and in need, all who bring to this place the offering of their hearts. May our worship here lead us to fulfill our words and our hopes with acts of kindness, peace, and love. Amen.

From Psalm 84

מַה־יְּדִידוֹת מִשְׁכְּנוֹתֶיךָ, יְהֹוָה צְבָאוֹת!
נִכְסְפָה וְגַם־כָּלְתָה נַפְשִׁי לְחַצְרוֹת יְהֹוָה,
לִבִּי וּבְשָׂרִי יְרַנְּנוּ אֶל אֵל־חָי.

How lovely are Your dwelling places, God of all being!
My soul longs and yearns for the courts of my God;
my heart and flesh sing for joy to the living God.

גַּם־צִפּוֹר מָצְאָה בַיִת, וּדְרוֹר קֵן לָהּ
אֲשֶׁר־שָׁתָה אֶפְרֹחֶיהָ, אֶת־מִזְבְּחוֹתֶיךָ,
יְהֹוָה צְבָאוֹת, מַלְכִּי וֵאלֹהָי.

As the sparrow finds a home, and the swallow has a nest
where she rears her young,
so do I seek out Your altars,
God of all being, my Sovereign God.

אַשְׁרֵי יוֹשְׁבֵי בֵיתֶךָ, עוֹד יְהַלְלוּךָ סֶּלָה.
אַשְׁרֵי אָדָם עוֹז־לוֹ בָךְ, מְסִלּוֹת בִּלְבָבָם.

Happy are those who dwell in Your house;
they will sing Your praise for ever.
Happy are those who find strength in You;
their hearts are highways leading to Your presence.

עֹבְרֵי בְּעֵמֶק הַבָּכָא מַעְיָן יְשִׁיתוּהוּ, גַּם־בְּרָכוֹת יַעְטֶה מוֹרֶה.
יֵלְכוּ מֵחַיִל אֶל־חָיִל, יֵרָאֶה אֶל־אֱלֹהִים בְּצִיּוֹן.

When they pass through the driest of valleys,
they find it a place of springs; the rain blesses it with pools.
They go from strength to strength; they behold God in Zion.

כִּי טוֹב־יוֹם בַּחֲצֵרֶיךָ מֵאָלֶף.

בָּחַרְתִּי הִסְתּוֹפֵף בְּבֵית אֱלֹהַי, מִדּוּר בְּאָהֳלֵי־רֶשַׁע.

One day in Your courts is better than a thousand elsewhere.
*And better it is to wait at the doorstep of Your house
than be an honored guest among the wicked.*

כִּי שֶׁמֶשׁ וּמָגֵן יְהֹוָה אֱלֹהִים, חֵן וְכָבוֹד יִתֵּן יְהֹוָה.

לֹא יִמְנַע־טוֹב לַהֹלְכִים בְּתָמִים.

יְהֹוָה צְבָאוֹת, אַשְׁרֵי אָדָם בֹּטֵחַ בָּךְ!

For the Eternal God is a sun and a shield;
God gives grace and glory.

No good is withheld from those who walk uprightly.
God of all being, happy is the one who trusts in You!

◆ ◆

We have come together to strengthen our bonds with our people
Israel. Like Jews of generations past, we celebrate the grandeur of
creation. Like Jews of every age, we echo our people's ancient call
for justice.
Our celebration is a sharing of memory and hope.

We are Jews, but each of us is unique. We stand apart and alone,
with differing feelings and insights. And yet we are not entirely
alone and separate, for we are children of one people and one
heritage.
*Our celebration unites many separate selves
into a single chorus.*

And we are one in search of life's meaning. All of us know despair
and exaltation; all bear burdens; all have moments of weakness
and times of strength; all sing songs of sorrow and love.
May our celebration bring us strength along our way.

In this circle of hope, in the presence of the sacred, may the heart come to know itself and its best, finding a fresh impulse to love the good.

May our celebration lead us to work for the good; and may this Shabbat give strength to us and to our people Israel.

◆ ◆

הִנֵּה מַה־טּוֹב וּמַה־

נָּעִים שֶׁבֶת אַחִים גַּם־יָחַד.

How good it is, and how pleasant,
when we dwell together in unity.

◆ ◆

Many are the generations of Israel, and in every age we have sought the living God through Sabbath rest and worship. This time and place hold the power to increase our joy in the Eternal. O God, even as we seek You in the sanctuary, help us to know that Your glory fills all space; make us understand that You are with us at all times, if we but open our minds to You.

We feel the presence of Your spirit in our homes and on our ways; we see the beauty of Your creation in mountain, sea, and sky, and in the human form; we hear You in the silence of our own hearts speaking the truths the heart knows.

May we be Your witness to the world,
Your messenger to all the earth.

*May we show forth Your image within us,
the divine spark that makes us human.*

All rise

READER'S KADDISH   חצי קדיש

יִתְגַּדַּל וְיִתְקַדַּשׁ שְׁמֵהּ רַבָּא בְּעָלְמָא דִי־בְרָא כִרְעוּתֵהּ,

וְיַמְלִיךְ מַלְכוּתֵהּ בְּחַיֵּיכוֹן וּבְיוֹמֵיכוֹן וּבְחַיֵּי

דְכָל־בֵּית יִשְׂרָאֵל, בַּעֲגָלָא וּבִזְמַן קָרִיב, וְאִמְרוּ: אָמֵן.

יְהֵא שְׁמֵהּ רַבָּא מְבָרַךְ לְעָלַם וּלְעָלְמֵי עָלְמַיָּא.

יִתְבָּרַךְ וְיִשְׁתַּבַּח, וְיִתְפָּאַר וְיִתְרוֹמַם וְיִתְנַשֵּׂא, וְיִתְהַדָּר

וְיִתְעַלֶּה וְיִתְהַלָּל שְׁמֵהּ דְּקוּדְשָׁא, בְּרִיךְ הוּא,

לְעֵלָּא מִן־כָּל־בִּרְכָתָא וְשִׁירָתָא, תֻּשְׁבְּחָתָא וְנֶחֱמָתָא

דַּאֲמִירָן בְּעָלְמָא, וְאִמְרוּ: אָמֵן.

Yit-ga-dal v'yit-ka-dash sh'mei ra-ba b'al-ma di-v'ra chir-u-tei, v'yam-lich mal-chu-tei b'cha-yei-chon u-v'yo-mei-chon u-v'cha-yei d'chol beit Yis-ra-eil, ba-a-ga-la u-viz-man ka-riv, v'im'ru: A-mein.

Y'hei sh'mei ra-ba m'va-rach l'a-lam u-l'al-mei al-ma-ya.

Yit-ba-rach v'yish-ta-bach v'yit-pa-ar, v'yit-ro-mam, v'yit-na-sei, v'yit-ha-dar, v'yit-a-leh, v'yit-ha-lal sh'mei d'kud'sha, b'rich hu,

L'ei-la min kol bir-cha-ta v'shi-ra-ta, tush-b'cha-ta v'neh-cheh-ma-ta da-a-mi-ran b'al-ma, v'im'ru: A-mein.

Let the glory of God be extolled, let God's great name be hallowed in the world whose creation God willed. May God's reign begin in our own day, our own lives, and the life of all Israel, and let us say: Amen.

Let God's great name be praised for ever and ever.

Let the name of the Holy One, the Blessed One, be glorified, exalted, and honored, though God is beyond all the praises, songs, and adorations that we can utter, and let us say: Amen.

The Sh'ma and Its Blessings   שמע וברכותיה

בָּרְכוּ אֶת־יְיָ הַמְבֹרָךְ!

Praise the One to whom praise is due!

בָּרוּךְ יְיָ הַמְבֹרָךְ לְעוֹלָם וָעֶד!

Praised be the One to whom praise is due, now and for ever!

CREATION   מעריב ערבים

בָּרוּךְ אַתָּה יְיָ, אֱלֹהֵינוּ מֶלֶךְ הָעוֹלָם,

אֲשֶׁר בִּדְבָרוֹ מַעֲרִיב עֲרָבִים, בְּחָכְמָה פּוֹתֵחַ שְׁעָרִים,

וּבִתְבוּנָה מְשַׁנֶּה עִתִּים, וּמַחֲלִיף אֶת־הַזְּמַנִּים,

וּמְסַדֵּר אֶת־הַכּוֹכָבִים בְּמִשְׁמְרוֹתֵיהֶם בָּרָקִיעַ כִּרְצוֹנוֹ.

בּוֹרֵא יוֹם וָלָיְלָה, גּוֹלֵל אוֹר מִפְּנֵי חֹשֶׁךְ וְחֹשֶׁךְ מִפְּנֵי אוֹר,

וּמַעֲבִיר יוֹם וּמֵבִיא לָיְלָה, וּמַבְדִּיל בֵּין יוֹם וּבֵין לָיְלָה,

יְיָ צְבָאוֹת שְׁמוֹ.

אֵל חַי וְקַיָּם, תָּמִיד יִמְלוֹךְ עָלֵינוּ לְעוֹלָם וָעֶד!

בָּרוּךְ אַתָּה יְיָ, הַמַּעֲרִיב עֲרָבִים.

° As day departs, as the dark of night descends, we lift our eyes to the heavens. In awe and wonder our hearts cry out:

Eternal God, how majestic is Your name in all the earth!

A vast universe: who can know it? What mind can fathom it? We look out to the endless suns and ask: What are we, what are our dreams and our hopes?

What are we, that You are mindful of us?
What are we, that You should care for us?

° This signifies that the English is a variation on the theme of the Hebrew.

And yet within us abides a measure of Your spirit. You are remote, but, oh, how near! Ordering the stars in the vast solitudes of the dark, yet whispering in the mind that You are closer than the air we breathe. With love and awe we turn to You, and in the dark of evening seek the light of Your presence.

For You have made us little less than divine,
and crowned us with glory and honor!

REVELATION   אהבת עולם

אַהֲבַת עוֹלָם בֵּית יִשְׂרָאֵל עַמְּךָ אָהָבְתָּ. תּוֹרָה וּמִצְוֹת, חֻקִּים
וּמִשְׁפָּטִים אוֹתָנוּ לִמַּדְתָּ. עַל-כֵּן, יְיָ אֱלֹהֵינוּ, בְּשָׁכְבֵּנוּ
וּבְקוּמֵנוּ נָשִׂיחַ בְּחֻקֶּיךָ, וְנִשְׂמַח בְּדִבְרֵי תוֹרָתֶךָ וּבְמִצְוֹתֶיךָ
לְעוֹלָם וָעֶד. כִּי הֵם חַיֵּינוּ וְאוֹרֶךְ יָמֵינוּ, וּבָהֶם נֶהְגֶּה יוֹמָם
וָלָיְלָה. וְאַהֲבָתְךָ אַל-תָּסוּר מִמֶּנּוּ לְעוֹלָמִים!
בָּרוּךְ אַתָּה יְיָ, אוֹהֵב עַמּוֹ יִשְׂרָאֵל.

° One and Only God, You have made each of us unique, and formed us to be united in one family of life. Be with us, Eternal One, as we seek to unite our lives with Your power and Your love.

We proclaim now Your Oneness and our own hope for unity;
we acclaim Your creative power in the universe and in
ourselves, the Law that binds world to world and heart to
heart:

◆ ◆

שְׁמַע יִשְׂרָאֵל יְהוָה אֱלֹהֵינוּ יְהוָה אֶחָד!
Sh'ma Yisrael: Adonai Eloheinu, Adonai Echad!

Hear, O Israel: the Eternal One is our God,
the Eternal God alone!

בָּרוּךְ שֵׁם כְּבוֹד מַלְכוּתוֹ לְעוֹלָם וָעֶד!
Baruch shem k'vod malchuto l'olam va-ed!

Blessed is God's glorious majesty for ever and ever!

All are seated

36

וְאָהַבְתָּ אֵת יְהֹוָה אֱלֹהֶיךָ בְּכָל־לְבָבְךָ וּבְכָל־נַפְשְׁךָ וּבְכָל־מְאֹדֶךָ:
וְהָיוּ הַדְּבָרִים הָאֵלֶּה אֲשֶׁר אָנֹכִי מְצַוְּךָ הַיּוֹם עַל־לְבָבֶךָ:
וְשִׁנַּנְתָּם לְבָנֶיךָ וְדִבַּרְתָּ בָּם בְּשִׁבְתְּךָ בְּבֵיתֶךָ וּבְלֶכְתְּךָ בַדֶּרֶךְ
וּבְשָׁכְבְּךָ וּבְקוּמֶךָ: וּקְשַׁרְתָּם לְאוֹת עַל־יָדֶךָ וְהָיוּ לְטֹטָפֹת בֵּין
עֵינֶיךָ: וּכְתַבְתָּם עַל־מְזוּזֹת בֵּיתֶךָ וּבִשְׁעָרֶיךָ:

V'a-hav-ta et Adonai eh-lo-heh-cha b'chol l'va-v'cha u-v'chol naf-sh'cha u-v'chol m'o-deh-cha. V'ha-yu ha-d'va-rim ha-ei-leh a-sher a-no-chi m'tza-v'cha ha-yom al l'va-veh-cha. V'shi-nan-tam l'va-neh-cha v'di-bar-ta bam b'shiv-t'cha b'vei-teh-cha u-v'lech-t'cha va-deh-rech u-v'shoch-b'cha u-v'ku-meh-cha. U-k'shar-tam l'oht al ya-deh-cha v'ha-yu l'toh-ta-foht bein ei-neh-cha; u-ch'tav-tam al m'zu-zoht bei-teh-cha u-vi-sh'a-reh-cha.

> *You shall love the Eternal One, your God, with all your heart, with all your mind, with all your being. Set these words, which I command you this day, upon your heart. Teach them faithfully to your children; speak of them in your home and on your way, when you lie down and when you rise up. Bind them as a sign upon your hand; let them be a symbol before your eyes; inscribe them on the doorposts of your house, and on your gates.*

לְמַעַן תִּזְכְּרוּ וַעֲשִׂיתֶם אֶת־כָּל־מִצְוֹתָי וִהְיִיתֶם קְדֹשִׁים
לֵאלֹהֵיכֶם: אֲנִי יְהֹוָה אֱלֹהֵיכֶם אֲשֶׁר הוֹצֵאתִי אֶתְכֶם
מֵאֶרֶץ מִצְרַיִם לִהְיוֹת לָכֶם לֵאלֹהִים. אֲנִי יְהֹוָה אֱלֹהֵיכֶם:

L'ma-an tiz-k'ru va-a-si-tem et kol mitz-vo-tai, vi-h'yi-tem k'doh-shim lei-lo-hei-chem. Ani Adonai eh-lo-hei-chem a-sher ho-tzei-ti et-chem mei-eh-retz mitz-ra-yim li-h'yoht la-chem lei-lo-him. Ani Adonai eh-lo-hei-chem.

> *Be mindful of all My Mitzvot, and do them: so shall you consecrate yourselves to your God. I am your Eternal God who led you out of Egypt to be your God; I am your Eternal God.*

REDEMPTION

גְּאוּלָה

אֱמֶת וֶאֱמוּנָה כָּל־זֹאת, וְקַיָּם עָלֵינוּ כִּי הוּא יְיָ אֱלֹהֵינוּ וְאֵין זוּלָתוֹ, וַאֲנַחְנוּ יִשְׂרָאֵל עַמּוֹ.

הַפּוֹדֵנוּ מִיַּד מְלָכִים, מַלְכֵּנוּ הַגּוֹאֲלֵנוּ מִכַּף כָּל־הֶעָרִיצִים.

הָעֹשֶׂה גְדֹלוֹת עַד אֵין חֵקֶר, וְנִפְלָאוֹת עַד־אֵין מִסְפָּר.

הַשָּׂם נַפְשֵׁנוּ בַּחַיִּים, וְלֹא־נָתַן לַמּוֹט רַגְלֵנוּ.

הָעֹשֶׂה לָּנוּ נִסִּים בְּפַרְעֹה, אוֹתוֹת וּמוֹפְתִים בְּאַדְמַת בְּנֵי חָם.

וַיּוֹצֵא אֶת־עַמּוֹ יִשְׂרָאֵל מִתּוֹכָם לְחֵרוּת עוֹלָם.

וְרָאוּ בָנָיו וּבְנוֹתָיו גְּבוּרָתוֹ; שִׁבְּחוּ וְהוֹדוּ לִשְׁמוֹ. וּמַלְכוּתוֹ בְּרָצוֹן קִבְּלוּ עֲלֵיהֶם. מֹשֶׁה וּמִרְיָם וּבְנֵי יִשְׂרָאֵל לְךָ עָנוּ שִׁירָה בְּשִׂמְחָה רַבָּה,

וְאָמְרוּ כֻלָּם:

° In a world torn by violence and pain, a world far from wholeness, a world waiting still to be redeemed, give us, O Source of good, the courage to say: There is one God in heaven and earth.

The high heavens declare Your glory; may earth reveal Your justice and Your love.

From Egypt, the house of bondage, we were delivered; at Sinai, amid peals of thunder, we bound ourselves to Your purpose. Inspired by prophets and instructed by sages, we survived oppression and exile, time and again overcoming the forces that would have destroyed us.

Our failings are many—our faults are great—yet it has been our glory to bear witness to our God, and to keep alive in dark ages the vision of a world redeemed.

May this vision never fade; let us continue to work for the day when the nations will be one and at peace. Then shall we sing with one accord, as Israel sang at the shores of the Sea:

מִי־כָמֹכָה בָּאֵלִם, יְהֹוָה? מִי כָּמֹכָה, נֶאְדָּר בַּקֹּדֶשׁ,
נוֹרָא תְהִלֹּת, עֹשֵׂה פֶלֶא?
מַלְכוּתְךָ רָאוּ בָנֶיךָ, בּוֹקֵעַ יָם לִפְנֵי מֹשֶׁה; זֶה אֵלִי!
עָנוּ וְאָמְרוּ: יְהֹוָה יִמְלֹךְ לְעֹלָם וָעֶד!
וְנֶאֱמַר: כִּי־פָדָה יְיָ אֶת־יַעֲקֹב, וּגְאָלוֹ מִיַּד חָזָק
מִמֶּנּוּ. בָּרוּךְ אַתָּה יְיָ, גָּאַל יִשְׂרָאֵל.

Mi cha-mo-cha ba-ei-lim, Adonai? Mi ka-mo-cha, ne-dar ba-ko-
desh, no-ra t'hi-loht, o-sei feh-leh?
Mal-chu-t'cha ra-u va-neh-cha, bo-kei-a yam lif-nei Mo-sheh; zeh
ei-li! a-nu v'am-ru: Adonai yim-loch l'o-lam va-ed.
V'neh-eh-mar: Ki fa-da Adonai et Ya-a-kov, u-g'a-lo mi-yad cha-zak
mi-meh-nu. Ba-ruch a-ta Adonai, ga-al Yis-ra-el.

Who is like You, Eternal One, among the gods that are worshipped?
Who is like You, majestic in holiness, awesome in splendor, doing
wonders?

In their escape from the sea, Your children saw Your sovereign might displayed. This is my God! they cried. The Eternal One will reign for ever
and ever

And it has been said: The Eternal One delivered Jacob, and redeemed us
from the hand of one stronger than ourselves. We praise You, Eternal
One, Redeemer of Israel.

DIVINE PROVIDENCE   הַשְׁכִּיבֵנוּ

הַשְׁכִּיבֵנוּ, יְיָ אֱלֹהֵינוּ, לְשָׁלוֹם, וְהַעֲמִידֵנוּ, מַלְכֵּנוּ, לְחַיִּים.
וּפְרֹשׂ עָלֵינוּ סֻכַּת שְׁלוֹמֶךָ, וְתַקְּנֵנוּ בְּעֵצָה טוֹבָה מִלְּפָנֶיךָ,
וְהוֹשִׁיעֵנוּ לְמַעַן שְׁמֶךָ, וְהָגֵן בַּעֲדֵנוּ. וְהָסֵר מֵעָלֵינוּ אוֹיֵב דֶּבֶר
וְחֶרֶב וְרָעָב וְיָגוֹן; וְהָסֵר שָׂטָן מִלְּפָנֵינוּ וּמֵאַחֲרֵינוּ, וּבְצֵל
כְּנָפֶיךָ תַּסְתִּירֵנוּ, כִּי אֵל שׁוֹמְרֵנוּ וּמַצִּילֵנוּ אָתָּה, כִּי אֵל מֶלֶךְ
חַנּוּן וְרַחוּם אָתָּה. וּשְׁמוֹר צֵאתֵנוּ וּבוֹאֵנוּ לְחַיִּים וּלְשָׁלוֹם
מֵעַתָּה וְעַד עוֹלָם. בָּרוּךְ אַתָּה יְיָ, הַפּוֹרֵשׂ סֻכַּת שָׁלוֹם עָלֵינוּ,
וְעַל־כָּל־עַמּוֹ־יִשְׂרָאֵל, וְעַל יְרוּשָׁלָיִם.

° Let there be love and understanding among us; let peace and friendship be our shelter from life's storms. Eternal God, help us to walk with good companions, to live with hope in our hearts and eternity in our thoughts, that we may lie down in peace and rise up to find our hearts waiting to do Your will.

We praise You, Guardian of Israel, whose love gives light to all the world.

O God of Israel, may our worship on this day help us to grow in loyalty to our covenant with You and to the way of life it demands: the way of gentleness and justice, the path of truth and of peace.

THE COVENANT OF SHABBAT   וְשָׁמְרוּ

וְשָׁמְרוּ בְנֵי־יִשְׂרָאֵל אֶת־הַשַּׁבָּת, לַעֲשׂוֹת אֶת־הַשַּׁבָּת לְדֹרֹתָם
בְּרִית עוֹלָם. בֵּינִי וּבֵין בְּנֵי יִשְׂרָאֵל אוֹת הִיא לְעֹלָם, כִּי־שֵׁשֶׁת
יָמִים עָשָׂה יְהוָה אֶת־הַשָּׁמַיִם וְאֶת־הָאָרֶץ, וּבַיּוֹם הַשְּׁבִיעִי
שָׁבַת וַיִּנָּפַשׁ.

V'sham'ru v'nei Yis-ra-el et ha-sha-bat, la-a-soht et ha-sha-bat l'doh-ro-tam, b'rit o-lam. Bei-ni u-vein b'nei Yis-ra-el ot hi l'o-lam, ki shei-shet ya-mim a-sa A-do-nai et ha-sha-ma-yim v'et ha-a-rets, u-va-yom ha-sh'vi-i sha-vat va-yi-na-fash.

The people of Israel shall keep the Sabbath, observing the Sabbath in every generation as a covenant for all time. It is a sign for ever between Me and the people of Israel, for in six days the Eternal God made heaven and earth, taking rest and refreshment on the seventh day.

MEDITATION

Prayer invites God to let the Divine Presence suffuse our spirits, to let the Divine will prevail in our lives. Prayer cannot bring water to parched fields, nor mend a broken bridge, nor rebuild a ruined city; but prayer can water an arid soul, mend a broken heart, and rebuild a weakened will.

All rise

T'filah   תפלה

אֲדֹנָי שְׂפָתַי תִּפְתָּח וּפִי יַגִּיד תְּהִלָּתֶךָ:

Eternal God, open my lips, that my mouth may declare Your glory.

GOD OF ALL GENERATIONS   אבות ואמהות

בָּרוּךְ אַתָּה יְיָ, אֱלֹהֵינוּ וֵאלֹהֵי אֲבוֹתֵינוּ וְאִמּוֹתֵינוּ:

אֱלֹהֵי אַבְרָהָם, אֱלֹהֵי יִצְחָק, וֵאלֹהֵי יַעֲקֹב.

אֱלֹהֵי שָׂרָה, אֱלֹהֵי רִבְקָה, אֱלֹהֵי לֵאָה, וֵאלֹהֵי רָחֵל.

הָאֵל הַגָּדוֹל הַגִּבּוֹר וְהַנּוֹרָא, אֵל עֶלְיוֹן,

גּוֹמֵל חֲסָדִים טוֹבִים וְקוֹנֵה הַכֹּל, וְזוֹכֵר חַסְדֵי אָבוֹת וְאִמָּהוֹת,

וּמֵבִיא גְאֻלָּה לִבְנֵי בְנֵיהֶם, לְמַעַן שְׁמוֹ בְּאַהֲבָה.

מֶלֶךְ עוֹזֵר וּמוֹשִׁיעַ וּמָגֵן.

בָּרוּךְ אַתָּה יְיָ, מָגֵן אַבְרָהָם וְעֶזְרַת שָׂרָה.

Ba-ruch a-ta Adonai, Eh-lo-hei-nu vei-lo-hei a-vo-tei-nu v'i-mo-tei-nu: Eh-lo-hei Av-ra-ham, eh-lo-hei Yitz-chak, vei-lo-hei Ya-a-kov. Eh-lo-hei Sa-rah, eh-lo-hei Riv-kah, eh-lo-hei Lei-ah, vei-lo-hei Ra-cheil. Ha-eil ha-ga-dol ha-gi-bor v'ha-no-ra, eil el-yon. Go-meil cha-sa-dim toh-vim, v'ko-nei ha-kol, v'zo-cheir chas-dei a-voht v'i-ma-hoht, u-mei-vi g'u-la li-v'nei v'nei-hem, l'ma-an sh'mo, b'a-ha-vah. Meh-lech o-zeir u-mo-shi-a u-ma-gein. Ba-ruch a-ta Adonai, ma-gein Av-ra-ham v'ez-rat Sa-rah.

° Source of all being, we turn to You as did our people in ancient days. They beheld You in the heavens; they felt You in their hearts; they sought You in their lives.

Now their quest is ours. Help us, O God, to see the wonder of being. Give us the courage to search for truth. Teach us the path to a better life. So shall we, by our lives and our labors, bring nearer to realization the great hope inherited from ages past, for a world transformed by liberty, justice, and peace.

41

Shabbat Evening Service II

GOD'S POWER   גבורות

אַתָּה גִבּוֹר לְעוֹלָם, אֲדֹנָי, מְחַיֵּה הַכֹּל אַתָּה, רַב לְהוֹשִׁיעַ.

מְכַלְכֵּל חַיִּים בְּחֶסֶד, מְחַיֵּה הַכֹּל בְּרַחֲמִים רַבִּים.

סוֹמֵךְ נוֹפְלִים, וְרוֹפֵא חוֹלִים, וּמַתִּיר אֲסוּרִים, וּמְקַיֵּם אֱמוּנָתוֹ

לִישֵׁנֵי עָפָר. מִי כָמוֹךָ בַּעַל גְּבוּרוֹת, וּמִי דּוֹמֶה לָּךְ,

מֶלֶךְ מֵמִית וּמְחַיֶּה וּמַצְמִיחַ יְשׁוּעָה?

וְנֶאֱמָן אַתָּה לְהַחֲיוֹת הַכֹּל. בָּרוּךְ אַתָּה יְיָ, מְחַיֵּה הַכֹּל.

A-ta gi-bor l'o-lam, Adonai, m'cha-yei ha-kol a-ta, rav l'ho-shi-a.
M'chal-keil cha-yim b'cheh-sed, m'cha-yei ha-kol b'ra-cha-mim
ra-bim. So-meich no-f'lim, v'ro-fei cho-lim, u-ma-tir a-su-rim,
u-m'ka-yeim eh-mu-na-toh li-shei-nei a-far. Mi cha-mo-cha ba-al
g'vu-roht, u-mi doh-meh lach, meh-lech mei-mit u-m'cha-yeh
u-matz-mi-ach y'shu-a?
V'neh-eh-man a-ta l'ha-cha-yoht ha-kol, Ba-ruch a-ta Adonai,
m'cha-yei ha-kol.

° Your might, O God, is everlasting;

    Help us to use our strength for good.

You are the Source of life and blessing;

    Help us to choose life for ourselves and our children.

You are the support of the falling;

    Help us to lift up the fallen.

You are the Author of freedom;

    Help us to free the captive.

You are our hope in death as in life.

    Help us to keep faith with those who sleep in the dust.

Your might, O God, is everlasting;

    Help us to use our strength for good.

THE HOLINESS OF GOD   קדושת השם

אַתָּה קָדוֹשׁ וְשִׁמְךָ קָדוֹשׁ, וּקְדוֹשִׁים בְּכָל־יוֹם יְהַלְלוּךָ סֶּלָה.
בָּרוּךְ אַתָּה יְיָ, הָאֵל הַקָּדוֹשׁ.

° A time can come to us when our hearts are filled with awe:
suddenly the noise of life will be stilled, as our eyes open to a world
just beyond the border of our minds. All at once there is a glory
in our souls! הָאֵל הַקָּדוֹשׁ!—The Holy God!

All are seated

MOST PRECIOUS OF DAYS   ישמחו

יִשְׂמְחוּ בְמַלְכוּתְךָ שׁוֹמְרֵי שַׁבָּת וְקוֹרְאֵי עֹנֶג. עַם מְקַדְּשֵׁי שְׁבִיעִי
כֻּלָּם יִשְׂבְּעוּ וְיִתְעַנְּגוּ מִטּוּבֶךָ. וְהַשְׁבִיעִי רָצִיתָ בּוֹ וְקִדַּשְׁתּוֹ.
חֶמְדַּת יָמִים אוֹתוֹ קָרֵאתָ, זֵכֶר לְמַעֲשֵׂה בְרֵאשִׁית.

Yis-m'chu v'ma-l'chu-t'cha sho-m'rei shabbat v'ko-r'ei o-neg. Am
m'ka-d'shei sh'vi-i ku-lam yis-b'u v'yit-a-n'gu mi-tu-veh-cha. V'ha-
sh'vi-i ra-tzi-ta bo v'ki-dash-toh. Chem-dat ya-mim o-toh ka-ra-ta,
zei-cher l'ma-a-sei v'rei-sheet.

Those who keep the Sabbath and call it a delight shall rejoice in
Your Presence. All who hallow the seventh day shall be gladdened
by Your goodness. This day is Israel's festival of the spirit, sanctified and blessed by You, the most precious of days, a symbol of
the joy of creation.

◆ ◆

THE HOLINESS OF SHABBAT   קְדוּשַׁת הַיּוֹם

אֱלֹהֵינוּ וֵאלֹהֵי אֲבוֹתֵינוּ וְאִמּוֹתֵינוּ, רְצֵה בִמְנוּחָתֵנוּ.

קַדְּשֵׁנוּ בְּמִצְוֹתֶיךָ וְתֵן חֶלְקֵנוּ בְּתוֹרָתֶךָ. שַׂבְּעֵנוּ מִטּוּבֶךָ,

וְשַׂמְּחֵנוּ בִּישׁוּעָתֶךָ, וְטַהֵר לִבֵּנוּ לְעָבְדְּךָ בֶּאֱמֶת.

וְהַנְחִילֵנוּ, יְיָ אֱלֹהֵינוּ, בְּאַהֲבָה וּבְרָצוֹן שַׁבַּת קָדְשֶׁךָ,

וְיָנוּחוּ בָהּ יִשְׂרָאֵל מְקַדְּשֵׁי שְׁמֶךָ.

בָּרוּךְ אַתָּה יְיָ, מְקַדֵּשׁ הַשַּׁבָּת.

° *God of Israel, may our worship on this Sabbath bring us
near to all that is high and holy. May it bind the generations
in bonds of love and sharing, and unite us with our people
in common hope and faith. And through Sabbath rest and
worship, may we learn to find fulfillment and joy in the
vision of peace for all the world.*

WORSHIP   עֲבוֹדָה

רְצֵה, יְיָ אֱלֹהֵינוּ, בְּעַמְּךָ יִשְׂרָאֵל, וּתְפִלָּתָם בְּאַהֲבָה תְקַבֵּל,

וּתְהִי לְרָצוֹן תָּמִיד עֲבוֹדַת יִשְׂרָאֵל עַמֶּךָ.

בָּרוּךְ אַתָּה יְיָ, שֶׁאוֹתְךָ לְבַדְּךָ בְּיִרְאָה נַעֲבוֹד.

° You are with us in our prayer, in our love and our doubt, in our
longing to feel Your presence and do Your will. You are the still,
clear voice within us. Therefore, O God, when doubt troubles us,
when anxiety makes us tremble, and pain clouds the mind, we look
inward for the answer to our prayers. There may we find You, and
there find courage, insight, and endurance. And let our worship
bring us closer to one another, that all Israel, and all who seek You,
may find new strength for Your service.

THANKSGIVING · הודאה

מוֹדִים אֲנַחְנוּ לָךְ שָׁאַתָּה הוּא יְיָ אֱלֹהֵינוּ וֵאלֹהֵי אֲבוֹתֵינוּ
וְאִמּוֹתֵינוּ, אֱלֹהֵי כָל־בָּשָׂר, יוֹצְרֵנוּ יוֹצֵר בְּרֵאשִׁית.
בְּרָכוֹת וְהוֹדָאוֹת לְשִׁמְךָ הַגָּדוֹל וְהַקָּדוֹשׁ עַל־שֶׁהֶחֱיִיתָנוּ
וְקִיַּמְתָּנוּ.

כֵּן תְּחַיֵּנוּ וּתְקַיְּמֵנוּ, יְיָ אֱלֹהֵינוּ, וּתְאַמְּצֵנוּ לִשְׁמֹר חֻקֶּיךָ,
לַעֲשׂוֹת רְצוֹנֶךָ, וּלְעָבְדְּךָ בְּלֵבָב שָׁלֵם. בָּרוּךְ אֵל הַהוֹדָאוֹת.

° *Eternal Source of good, we give thanks for the numberless
gifts and blessings that fill our days: for life itself and its
endless variety; for all that sustains body and mind; for love
and friendship; for the delights of the senses; and for the
excellence of Your Torah, which deepens our life and
enriches our days.*

*Teach us, God of wonders, to work for a just and
compassionate society, where all may share Your gifts in the
joy of freedom.*

PEACE · ברכת שלום

שָׁלוֹם רָב עַל־יִשְׂרָאֵל עַמְּךָ, וְעַל־כָּל־הָעַמִּים, תָּשִׂים לְעוֹלָם.
Let Israel Your people, and all peoples, know peace for ever.

Let the great shofar of freedom be sounded for us and all peoples.
Let peace and freedom reign in all the world.

Let every wanderer come home from the bitterness of exile.
And may our eyes behold Your return to Zion in mercy.

Then will Jerusalem, the city of David, be the city of peace,
the joy of all the world.
The land of Israel and its people will see freedom and peace.

בָּרוּךְ אַתָּה יְיָ, עוֹשֵׂה הַשָּׁלוֹם.
We praise You, Eternal One, Source of peace.

45

Shabbat Evening Service II

MEDITATION

These quiet moments of Shabbat open my soul. Blessed with another week of life, I give thanks to the One who creates and sustains me.

For all the good I have known during the days that have passed, I am very grateful. I know that I have not always responded with my best effort, but often I did earnestly try. I have tried to give my family love and devotion, and I pray that I may grow more loving as the years pass.

Even as I regret my weaknesses, I rejoice in my accomplishments. Let these achievements, O God, lead to many others. May I be blessed on each Shabbat with the sense of having grown in goodness and compassion.

◆ ◆

יִהְיוּ לְרָצוֹן אִמְרֵי־פִי וְהֶגְיוֹן לִבִּי לְפָנֶיךָ, יְהֹוָה, צוּרִי וְגֹאֲלִי.

May the words of my mouth, and the meditations of my heart, be acceptable to You, O God, my Rock and my Redeemer.

◆

עֹשֶׂה שָׁלוֹם בִּמְרוֹמָיו, הוּא יַעֲשֶׂה שָׁלוֹם עָלֵינוּ
וְעַל־כָּל־יִשְׂרָאֵל, וְאִמְרוּ אָמֵן.

May the One who causes peace to reign in the high heavens let peace descend on us, on all Israel, and all the world.

◆ ◆

Pray as if everything depended on God;
act as if everything depended on you.
Who rise from prayer better people,
their prayer is answered.

The Service for the reading of Torah is on page 65

Aleinu is on page 73 or page 76

46

Shabbat Morning Service

The synagogue is the sanctuary of Israel. Born of our longing for the living God, it has been to Israel, throughout our wanderings, a visible token of the presence of God in our people's midst. Its beauty is the beauty of holiness; steadfast it has stood as the champion of justice, mercy, and peace.

Its truths are true for all people. Its love is a love for all people. Its God is the God of all people, as it has been said: My house shall be called a house of prayer for all peoples.

Let all the family of Israel, all who hunger for righteousness, all who seek the Eternal, find God here—and here find life!

מַה־טֹּבוּ אֹהָלֶיךָ, יַעֲקֹב, מִשְׁכְּנֹתֶיךָ יִשְׂרָאֵל!

וַאֲנִי, בְּרֹב חַסְדְּךָ אָבוֹא בֵיתֶךָ,

אֶשְׁתַּחֲוֶה אֶל־הֵיכַל קָדְשְׁךָ בְּיִרְאָתֶךָ.

יְהֹוָה, אָהַבְתִּי מְעוֹן בֵּיתֶךָ, וּמְקוֹם מִשְׁכַּן כְּבוֹדֶךָ.

וַאֲנִי אֶשְׁתַּחֲוֶה וְאֶכְרָעָה, אֶבְרְכָה לִפְנֵי־יְהֹוָה עֹשִׂי.

וַאֲנִי תְפִלָּתִי־לְךָ, יְהֹוָה, עֵת רָצוֹן.

אֱלֹהִים, בְּרָב־חַסְדֶּךָ, עֲנֵנִי בֶּאֱמֶת יִשְׁעֶךָ.

How lovely are your tents, O Jacob,
your dwelling-places, O Israel!
By Your abounding love, O God,
I enter your house;
with awe I worship in Your holy temple.
I love Your house, O Eternal One,
the dwelling-place of Your glory;
humbly do I worship You,
humbly seek blessing from God my Maker.
To You, Eternal One, goes my prayer:
may this be a time of Your favor.
In Your great love, O God,
answer me with Your saving truth.

MEDITATION

Each of us enters this sanctuary with a different need.

Some hearts are full of gratitude and joy:
They are overflowing with the happiness of love and the joy of life;
they are eager to confront the day, to make the world more fair;
they are recovering from illness or have escaped misfortune.
And we rejoice with them.

Some hearts ache with sorrow:
Disappointments weigh heavily upon them, and they have tasted
despair; families have been broken; loved ones lie on a bed of pain;
death has taken those whom they cherished.
May our presence and sympathy bring them comfort.

Some hearts are embittered:
They have sought answers in vain; ideals are mocked and
betrayed; life has lost its meaning and value.
May the knowledge that we too are searching, restore their hope
and give them courage to believe that not all is emptiness.

Some spirits hunger:
They long for friendship; they crave understanding;
they yearn for warmth.

May we in our common need and striving gain strength from
one another, as we share our joys, lighten each other's burdens,
and pray for the welfare of our community.

◆ ◆

Eternal One, You are our unfailing help. Darkness does not con-
ceal You from the eye of faith, nor do the forces of destruction
obscure Your presence. Above the fury of human evil and the
blows of chance You abide, the Eternal God. When pain and sorrow try our souls, grant us courage to meet them undismayed and
with faith that does not waver. Let not the tears that must come
to every eye blind us to Your goodness. Amen.

All rise

חצי קדיש

יִתְגַּדַּל וְיִתְקַדַּשׁ שְׁמֵהּ רַבָּא בְּעָלְמָא דִי־בְרָא כִרְעוּתֵהּ,
וְיַמְלִיךְ מַלְכוּתֵהּ בְּחַיֵּיכוֹן וּבְיוֹמֵיכוֹן וּבְחַיֵּי
דְכָל־בֵּית יִשְׂרָאֵל, בַּעֲגָלָא וּבִזְמַן קָרִיב, וְאִמְרוּ: אָמֵן.

יְהֵא שְׁמֵהּ רַבָּא מְבָרַךְ לְעָלַם וּלְעָלְמֵי עָלְמַיָּא.

יִתְבָּרַךְ וְיִשְׁתַּבַּח, וְיִתְפָּאַר וְיִתְרוֹמַם וְיִתְנַשֵּׂא, וְיִתְהַדָּר
וְיִתְעַלֶּה וְיִתְהַלָּל שְׁמֵהּ דְּקוּדְשָׁא, בְּרִיךְ הוּא,
לְעֵלָּא מִן־כָּל־בִּרְכָתָא וְשִׁירָתָא, תֻּשְׁבְּחָתָא וְנֶחֱמָתָא
דַּאֲמִירָן בְּעָלְמָא, וְאִמְרוּ: אָמֵן.

Yit-ga-dal v'yit-ka-dash sh'mei ra-ba b'al-ma di-v'ra chir-u-tei,
v'yam-lich mal-chu-tei b'cha-yei-chon u-v'yo-mei-chon u-v'cha-yei
d'chol beit Yis-ra-eil, ba-a-ga-la u-viz-man ka-riv, v'im'ru: A-mein.

Y'hei sh'mei ra-ba m'va-rach l'a-lam u-l'al-mei al-ma-ya.

Yit-ba-rach v'yish-ta-bach v'yit-pa-ar, v'yit-ro-mam, v'yit-na-sei,
v'yit-ha-dar, v'yit-a-leh, v'yit-ha-lal sh'mei d'kud'sha, b'rich hu,

L'ei-la min kol bir-cha-ta v'shi-ra-ta, tush-b'cha-ta v'neh-cheh-ma-ta
da-a-mi-ran b'al-ma, v'im'ru: A-mein.

Let the glory of God be extolled, let God's great name be hallowed in the
world whose creation God willed. May God's reign begin in our own day,
our own lives, and the life of all Israel, and let us say: Amen.

Let God's great name be praised for ever and ever.

Let the name of the Holy One, the Blessed One, be glorified, exalted, and
honored, though God is beyond all the praises, songs, and adorations that
we can utter, and let us say: Amen.

The Sh'ma and Its Blessings שמע וברכותיה

בָּרְכוּ אֶת־יְיָ הַמְבֹרָךְ!

Praise the One to whom praise is due!

בָּרוּךְ יְיָ הַמְבֹרָךְ לְעוֹלָם וָעֶד!

Praised be the One to whom praise is due, now and for ever!

CREATION יוצר

בָּרוּךְ אַתָּה יְיָ, אֱלֹהֵינוּ מֶלֶךְ הָעוֹלָם,
יוֹצֵר אוֹר וּבוֹרֵא חֹשֶׁךְ, עֹשֶׂה שָׁלוֹם וּבוֹרֵא אֶת־הַכֹּל.
הַמֵּאִיר לָאָרֶץ וְלַדָּרִים עָלֶיהָ בְּרַחֲמִים,
וּבְטוּבוֹ מְחַדֵּשׁ בְּכָל־יוֹם תָּמִיד מַעֲשֵׂה בְרֵאשִׁית.
מָה רַבּוּ מַעֲשֶׂיךָ יְיָ! כֻּלָּם בְּחָכְמָה עָשִׂיתָ, מָלְאָה הָאָרֶץ קִנְיָנֶךָ.
תִּתְבָּרַךְ, יְיָ אֱלֹהֵינוּ, עַל־שֶׁבַח מַעֲשֵׂה יָדֶיךָ,
וְעַל־מְאוֹרֵי־אוֹר שֶׁעָשִׂיתָ: יְפָאֲרוּךָ. סֶלָה.
בָּרוּךְ אַתָּה יְיָ, יוֹצֵר הַמְּאוֹרוֹת.

• Praised be our Eternal God, Ruler of the universe, whose mercy makes light to shine over the earth and all its inhabitants, and whose goodness renews day by day the work of creation.

How manifold are Your works, O God! In wisdom You have made them all. The heavens declare Your glory. The earth reveals Your creative power. You form light and darkness, bring harmony into nature, and peace to the human heart.

We praise You, Eternal One, Creator of light.

• The English is a paraphrase of the Hebrew.

REVELATION   אהבה רבה

אַהֲבָה רַבָּה אֲהַבְתָּנוּ, יְיָ אֱלֹהֵינוּ, חֶמְלָה גְדוֹלָה וִיתֵרָה חָמַלְתָּ
עָלֵינוּ. אָבִינוּ מַלְכֵּנוּ, בַּעֲבוּר אֲבוֹתֵינוּ וְאִמּוֹתֵינוּ שֶׁבָּטְחוּ בְךָ
וַתְּלַמְּדֵם חֻקֵּי חַיִּים, כֵּן תְּחָנֵּנוּ וּתְלַמְּדֵנוּ.

אָבִינוּ, הָאָב הָרַחֲמָן, הַמְרַחֵם, רַחֵם עָלֵינוּ וְתֵן בְּלִבֵּנוּ לְהָבִין
וּלְהַשְׂכִּיל, לִשְׁמֹעַ לִלְמֹד וּלְלַמֵּד, לִשְׁמֹר וְלַעֲשׂוֹת וּלְקַיֵּם
אֶת־כָּל־דִּבְרֵי תַלְמוּד תּוֹרָתֶךָ בְּאַהֲבָה.

וְהָאֵר עֵינֵינוּ בְּתוֹרָתֶךָ, וְדַבֵּק לִבֵּנוּ בְּמִצְוֹתֶיךָ, וְיַחֵד לְבָבֵנוּ
לְאַהֲבָה וּלְיִרְאָה אֶת־שְׁמֶךָ. וְלֹא־נֵבוֹשׁ לְעוֹלָם וָעֶד, כִּי בְשֵׁם
קָדְשְׁךָ הַגָּדוֹל וְהַנּוֹרָא בָּטָחְנוּ. נָגִילָה וְנִשְׂמְחָה בִּישׁוּעָתֶךָ, כִּי
אֵל פּוֹעֵל יְשׁוּעוֹת אָתָּה, וּבָנוּ בָחַרְתָּ וְקֵרַבְתָּנוּ לְשִׁמְךָ הַגָּדוֹל
סֶלָה בֶּאֱמֶת, לְהוֹדוֹת לְךָ וּלְיַחֶדְךָ בְּאַהֲבָה.
בָּרוּךְ אַתָּה יְיָ, הַבּוֹחֵר בְּעַמּוֹ יִשְׂרָאֵל בְּאַהֲבָה.

* Deep is Your love for us, abiding Your compassion. From of old
we have put our trust in You, and You have taught us the laws of
life. Be gracious now to us, that we may understand and fulfill the
teachings of Your word.

> *Enlighten our eyes in Your Torah, that we may cling to Your
> Mitzvot. Unite our hearts to love and revere Your name.*

> *We trust in You and rejoice in Your saving power, for You
> are the Source of our help. You have called us and drawn us
> near to You to serve You in faithfulness.*

> *Joyfully we lift up our voices and proclaim Your unity, O God
> who in love have called us to Your service!*

❖ ❖

שְׁמַע יִשְׂרָאֵל יְהֹוָה אֱלֹהֵינוּ יְהֹוָה אֶחָד!

Sh'ma Yisrael: Adonai Eloheinu, Adonai Echad!

Hear, O Israel: the Eternal One is our God,
the Eternal God alone!

בָּרוּךְ שֵׁם כְּבוֹד מַלְכוּתוֹ לְעוֹלָם וָעֶד!

Baruch shem k'vod malchuto l'olam va-ed!

Blessed is God's glorious majesty for ever and ever!

All are seated

וְאָהַבְתָּ אֵת יְהֹוָה אֱלֹהֶיךָ בְּכָל־לְבָבְךָ וּבְכָל־נַפְשְׁךָ וּבְכָל־מְאֹדֶךָ:
וְהָיוּ הַדְּבָרִים הָאֵלֶּה אֲשֶׁר אָנֹכִי מְצַוְּךָ הַיּוֹם עַל־לְבָבֶךָ:
וְשִׁנַּנְתָּם לְבָנֶיךָ וְדִבַּרְתָּ בָּם בְּשִׁבְתְּךָ בְּבֵיתֶךָ וּבְלֶכְתְּךָ בַדֶּרֶךְ
וּבְשָׁכְבְּךָ וּבְקוּמֶךָ: וּקְשַׁרְתָּם לְאוֹת עַל־יָדֶךָ וְהָיוּ לְטֹטָפֹת בֵּין
עֵינֶיךָ: וּכְתַבְתָּם עַל־מְזוּזֹת בֵּיתֶךָ וּבִשְׁעָרֶיךָ:

V'a-hav-ta et Adonai eh-lo-heh-cha b'chol l'va-v'cha u-v'chol naf-
sh'cha u-v'chol m'o-deh-cha. V'ha-yu ha-d'va-rim ha-ei-leh a-sher
a-no-chi m'tza-v'cha ha-yom al l'va-veh-cha. V'shi-nan-tam l'va-
neh-cha v'di-bar-ta bam b'shiv-t'cha b'vei-teh-cha u-v'lech-t'cha
va-deh-rech u-v'shoch-b'cha u-v'ku-meh-cha. U-k'shar-tam l'oht al
ya-deh-cha v'ha-yu l'toh-ta-foht bein ei-neh-cha; u-ch'tav-tam al
m'zu-zoht bei-teh-cha u-vi-sh'a-reh-cha.

*You shall love the Eternal One, your God, with all your
heart, with all your mind, with all your being. Set these
words, which I command you this day, upon your heart.
Teach them faithfully to your children; speak of them in your
home and on your way, when you lie down and when you
rise up. Bind them as a sign upon your hand; let them be a
symbol before your eyes; inscribe them on the doorposts of
your house, and on your gates.*

52

לְמַעַן תִּזְכְּרוּ וַעֲשִׂיתֶם אֶת־כָּל־מִצְוֹתָי וִהְיִיתֶם קְדֹשִׁים
לֵאלֹהֵיכֶם: אֲנִי יְהוָה אֱלֹהֵיכֶם אֲשֶׁר הוֹצֵאתִי אֶתְכֶם
מֵאֶרֶץ מִצְרַיִם לִהְיוֹת לָכֶם לֵאלֹהִים. אֲנִי יְהוָה אֱלֹהֵיכֶם:

L'ma-an tiz-k'ru va-a-si-tem et kol mitz-vo-tai, vi-h'yi-tem k'doh-shim
lei-lo-hei-chem. Ani Adonai eh-lo-hei-chem a-sher ho-tzei-ti
et-chem mei-eh-retz mitz-ra-yim li-h'yoht la-chem lei-lo-him. Ani
Adonai eh-lo-hei-chem.

Be mindful of all My Mitzvot, and do them: so shall you
consecrate yourselves to your God. I am your Eternal God
who led you out of Egypt to be your God; I am your Eternal
God.

REDEMPTION   גאולה

אֱמֶת וְיַצִּיב, וְאָהוּב וְחָבִיב, וְנוֹרָא וְאַדִּיר, וְטוֹב וְיָפֶה הַדָּבָר
הַזֶּה עָלֵינוּ לְעוֹלָם וָעֶד.

אֱמֶת, אֱלֹהֵי עוֹלָם מַלְכֵּנוּ, צוּר יַעֲקֹב מָגֵן יִשְׁעֵנוּ.

לְדֹר וָדֹר הוּא קַיָּם, וּשְׁמוֹ קַיָּם, וְכִסְאוֹ נָכוֹן,

וּמַלְכוּתוֹ וֶאֱמוּנָתוֹ לָעַד קַיָּמֶת. וּדְבָרָיו חָיִים וְקַיָּמִים,

נֶאֱמָנִים וְנֶחֱמָדִים, לָעַד וּלְעוֹלְמֵי עוֹלָמִים.

מִמִּצְרַיִם גְּאַלְתָּנוּ, יְיָ אֱלֹהֵינוּ, וּמִבֵּית עֲבָדִים פְּדִיתָנוּ.

עַל־זֹאת שִׁבְּחוּ אֲהוּבִים וְרוֹמְמוּ אֵל, וְנָתְנוּ יְדִידִים זְמִירוֹת

שִׁירוֹת וְתִשְׁבָּחוֹת, בְּרָכוֹת וְהוֹדָאוֹת לַמֶּלֶךְ, אֵל חַי וְקַיָּם.

רָם וְנִשָּׂא, גָּדוֹל וְנוֹרָא, מַשְׁפִּיל גֵּאִים וּמַגְבִּיהַּ שְׁפָלִים,

מוֹצִיא אֲסִירִים וּפוֹדֶה עֲנָוִים, וְעוֹזֵר דַּלִּים,

וְעוֹנֶה לְעַמּוֹ בְּעֵת שַׁוְּעָם אֵלָיו.

תְּהִלּוֹת לְאֵל עֶלְיוֹן, בָּרוּךְ הוּא וּמְבֹרָךְ. מֹשֶׁה וּמִרְיָם וּבְנֵי

יִשְׂרָאֵל לְךָ עָנוּ שִׁירָה בְּשִׂמְחָה רַבָּה, וְאָמְרוּ כֻלָּם:

53

• True and enduring are the words spoken by our prophets.
You are the living God;
Your word brings life and light to the soul.

You are the First and the Last:
besides You there is no redeemer or savior.

You are the strength of our life, the Power that saves us.
Your love and Your truth abide for ever.

You have been the help of our people in time of trouble;
You are our refuge in all generations.

Your power was manifest when we went free out of Egypt;
in every liberation from bondage we see it.

May Your law of freedom rule the hearts of all Your children,
and Your law of justice unite them in friendship.
May the righteous of all nations rejoice in Your love
and triumph by Your power.

O God, our refuge and our hope, we glorify Your name now
as did our people in ancient days:

מִי־כָמֹֽכָה בָּאֵלִם, יְהֹוָה? מִי כָּמֹֽכָה, נֶאְדָּר בַּקֹּֽדֶשׁ,
נוֹרָא תְהִלֹּת, עֹֽשֵׂה פֶֽלֶא?
שִׁירָה חֲדָשָׁה שִׁבְּחוּ גְאוּלִים לְשִׁמְךָ עַל־שְׂפַת הַיָּם;
יַֽחַד כֻּלָּם הוֹדוּ וְהִמְלִֽיכוּ וְאָמְרוּ: יְהֹוָה יִמְלֹךְ לְעֹלָם וָעֶד.

Mi cha-mo-cha ba-ei-lim, Adonai? Mi ka-mo-cha, ne-dar ba-ko-
desh, no-ra t'hi-loht, o-sei feh-leh?

Shi-ra cha-da-sha shi-b'chu g'u-lim l'shi-m'cha al s'fat ha-yam;
ya-chad ku-lam ho-du v'him-li-chu v'am'ru: Adonai Yim-loch l'o-lam
va-ed!

Who is like You, Eternal One, among the gods that are worshipped? Who is like You, majestic in holiness, awesome in splendor, doing wonders?

A new song the redeemed sang to Your name. At the shore of the sea, saved from destruction, they proclaimed Your sovereign power: The Eternal One will reign for ever and ever!

צוּר יִשְׂרָאֵל, קוּמָה בְּעֶזְרַת יִשְׂרָאֵל,

וּפְדֵה כִנְאֻמֶךָ יְהוּדָה וְיִשְׂרָאֵל. גֹּאֲלֵנוּ יְיָ צְבָאוֹת שְׁמוֹ,

קְדוֹשׁ יִשְׂרָאֵל. בָּרוּךְ אַתָּה יְיָ, גָּאַל יִשְׂרָאֵל.

O Rock of Israel, come to Israel's help. Fulfill Your promise of redemption for Judah and Israel. Our Redeemer is God on High, the Holy One of Israel. We praise You, Eternal One, Redeemer of Israel.

All rise

T'filah תפלה

אֲדֹנָי שְׂפָתַי תִּפְתָּח וּפִי יַגִּיד תְּהִלָּתֶךָ׃

Eternal God, open my lips, that my mouth may declare Your glory.

GOD OF ALL GENERATIONS   אבות ואמהות

בָּרוּךְ אַתָּה יְיָ, אֱלֹהֵינוּ וֵאלֹהֵי אֲבוֹתֵינוּ וְאִמּוֹתֵינוּ׃

אֱלֹהֵי אַבְרָהָם, אֱלֹהֵי יִצְחָק, וֵאלֹהֵי יַעֲקֹב.

אֱלֹהֵי שָׂרָה, אֱלֹהֵי רִבְקָה, אֱלֹהֵי לֵאָה, וֵאלֹהֵי רָחֵל.

הָאֵל הַגָּדוֹל הַגִּבּוֹר וְהַנּוֹרָא, אֵל עֶלְיוֹן,

גּוֹמֵל חֲסָדִים טוֹבִים וְקוֹנֵה הַכֹּל, וְזוֹכֵר חַסְדֵי אָבוֹת וְאִמָּהוֹת,

וּמֵבִיא גְאֻלָּה לִבְנֵי בְנֵיהֶם, לְמַעַן שְׁמוֹ בְּאַהֲבָה.

מֶלֶךְ עוֹזֵר וּמוֹשִׁיעַ וּמָגֵן.

בָּרוּךְ אַתָּה יְיָ, מָגֵן אַבְרָהָם וְעֶזְרַת שָׂרָה.

Ba-ruch a-ta Adonai, Eh-lo-hei-nu vei-lo-hei a-vo-tei-nu v'i-mo-tei-nu: Eh-lo-hei Av-ra-ham, eh-lo-hei Yitz-chak, vei-lo-hei Ya-a-kov. Eh-lo-hei Sa-rah, eh-lo-hei Riv-kah, eh-lo-hei Lei-ah, vei-lo-hei Ra-cheil. Ha-eil ha-ga-dol ha-gi-bor v'ha-no-ra, eil el-yon. Go-meil cha-sa-dim toh-vim, v'ko-nei ha-kol, v'zo-cheir chas-dei a-voht v'i-ma-hoht, u-mei-vi g'u-la li-v'nei v'nei-hem, l'ma-an sh'mo, b'a-ha-vah. Meh-lech o-zeir u-mo-shi-a u-ma-gein. Ba-ruch a-ta Adonai, ma-gein Av-ra-ham v'ez-rat Sa-rah.

Praised be the Eternal One, our God, God of our fathers and our mothers, God of Abraham, God of Isaac, and God of Jacob, God of Sarah, God of Rebekah, God of Leah and God of Rachel, great, mighty, and exalted.

You bestow love and kindness on all Your children. You remember the devotion of ages past. In Your love, You bring redemption to their descendants for the sake of Your name.

You are our Ruler and Helper, our Savior and Protector. We praise You, Eternal One, Shield of Abraham, Protector of Sarah.

GOD'S POWER   גבורות

אַתָּה גִבּוֹר לְעוֹלָם, אֲדֹנָי, מְחַיֵּה הַכֹּל אַתָּה, רַב לְהוֹשִׁיעַ.
מְכַלְכֵּל חַיִּים בְּחֶסֶד, מְחַיֵּה הַכֹּל בְּרַחֲמִים רַבִּים.
סוֹמֵךְ נוֹפְלִים, וְרוֹפֵא חוֹלִים, וּמַתִּיר אֲסוּרִים, וּמְקַיֵּם אֱמוּנָתוֹ
לִישֵׁנֵי עָפָר. מִי כָמוֹךָ בַּעַל גְּבוּרוֹת, וּמִי דּוֹמֶה לָּךְ,
מֶלֶךְ מֵמִית וּמְחַיֶּה וּמַצְמִיחַ יְשׁוּעָה?
וְנֶאֱמָן אַתָּה לְהַחֲיוֹת הַכֹּל. בָּרוּךְ אַתָּה יְיָ, מְחַיֵּה הַכֹּל.

A-ta gi-bor l'o-lam, Adonai, m'cha-yei ha-kol a-ta, rav l'ho-shi-a.
M'chal-keil cha-yim b'cheh-sed, m'cha-yei ha-kol b'ra-cha-mim
ra-bim. So-meich no-f'lim, v'ro-fei cho-lim, u-ma-tir a-su-rim,
u-m'ka-yeim eh-mu-na-toh li-shei-nei a-far. Mi cha-mo-cha ba-al
g'vu-roht, u-mi doh-meh lach, meh-lech mei-mit u-m'cha-yeh
u-matz-mi-ach y'shu-a?

V'neh-eh-man a-ta l'ha-cha-yoht ha-kol, Ba-ruch a-ta Adonai,
m'cha-yei ha-kol.

Eternal is Your might, O God, and great is Your saving power. In
love You sustain the living; in Your great mercy, You sustain us
all. You uphold the falling and heal the sick; free the captive and
keep faith with Your children in death as in life.

> *Who is like You, Almighty God, Author of life and death,*
> *Source of salvation?*
> *We praise You, Eternal One, the Source of life.*

SANCTIFICATION   קְדוּשָׁה

נְקַדֵּשׁ אֶת־שִׁמְךָ בָּעוֹלָם, כְּשֵׁם שֶׁמַּקְדִּישִׁים אוֹתוֹ בִּשְׁמֵי מָרוֹם,
כַּכָּתוּב עַל־יַד נְבִיאֶךָ: וְקָרָא זֶה אֶל־זֶה וְאָמַר:

We sanctify Your name on earth, even as all things, to the ends of
time and space, proclaim Your holiness, and in the words of the
prophet we say:

קָדוֹשׁ, קָדוֹשׁ, קָדוֹשׁ יְהוָה צְבָאוֹת, מְלֹא כָל־הָאָרֶץ כְּבוֹדוֹ.

*Holy, Holy, Holy is God Most High! The whole earth is
ablaze with Your glory!*

אַדִּיר אַדִּירֵנוּ, יְהוָה אֲדֹנֵינוּ, מָה־אַדִּיר שִׁמְךָ בְּכָל־הָאָרֶץ!

Source of our strength, Sovereign God, how majestic is Your name
in all the earth!

בָּרוּךְ כְּבוֹד־יְהוָה מִמְּקוֹמוֹ.

Praised be the glory of God in heaven and earth.

אֶחָד הוּא אֱלֹהֵינוּ, הוּא אָבִינוּ, הוּא מַלְכֵּנוּ, הוּא מוֹשִׁיעֵנוּ;
וְהוּא יַשְׁמִיעֵנוּ בְּרַחֲמָיו לְעֵינֵי כָּל־חָי:

You alone are our God and our Creator; You are our Ruler and
our Helper; and in Your mercy You reveal Yourself in the sight
of all the living:

"אֲנִי יְהוָה אֱלֹהֵיכֶם"

I AM YOUR ETERNAL GOD!

יִמְלֹךְ יְהוָה לְעוֹלָם, אֱלֹהַיִךְ צִיּוֹן, לְדֹר וָדֹר. הַלְלוּיָהּ!

*The Eternal One shall reign for ever; your God, O Zion,
from generation to generation. Halleluyah!*

58

לְדוֹר וָדוֹר נַגִּיד גָּדְלֶךָ, וּלְנֵצַח נְצָחִים קְדֻשָּׁתְךָ נַקְדִּישׁ.
וְשִׁבְחֲךָ, אֱלֹהֵינוּ, מִפִּינוּ לֹא יָמוּשׁ לְעוֹלָם וָעֶד.
בָּרוּךְ אַתָּה יְיָ, הָאֵל הַקָּדוֹשׁ.

To all generations we will make known Your greatness, and to all
eternity proclaim Your holiness. Your praise, O God, shall never
depart from our lips.

We praise You, Eternal One, the holy God.

All are seated

THE HOLINESS OF SHABBAT   קדושת היום

וְשָׁמְרוּ בְנֵי־יִשְׂרָאֵל אֶת־הַשַּׁבָּת, לַעֲשׂוֹת אֶת־הַשַּׁבָּת לְדֹרֹתָם
בְּרִית עוֹלָם. בֵּינִי וּבֵין בְּנֵי יִשְׂרָאֵל אוֹת הִיא לְעֹלָם, כִּי־שֵׁשֶׁת
יָמִים עָשָׂה יְהוָה אֶת־הַשָּׁמַיִם וְאֶת־הָאָרֶץ, וּבַיּוֹם הַשְּׁבִיעִי
שָׁבַת וַיִּנָּפַשׁ.

V'sham'ru v'nei Yis-ra-el et ha-sha-bat, la-a-soht et ha-sha-bat
l'doh-ro-tam, b'rit o-lam. Bei-ni u-vein b'nei Yis-ra-el ot hi l'o-lam,
ki shei-shet ya-mim a-sa A-do-nai et ha-sha-ma-yim v'et ha-a-rets,
u-va-yom ha-sh'vi-i sha-vat va-yi-na-fash.

The people of Israel shall keep the Sabbath, observing the Sabbath
in every generation as a covenant for all time. It is a sign for ever
between Me and the people of Israel, for in six days the Eternal
God made heaven and earth, taking rest and refreshment on the
seventh day.

אֱלֹהֵינוּ וֵאלֹהֵי אֲבוֹתֵינוּ וְאִמּוֹתֵינוּ, רְצֵה בִמְנוּחָתֵנוּ.
קַדְּשֵׁנוּ בְּמִצְוֺתֶיךָ וְתֵן חֶלְקֵנוּ בְּתוֹרָתֶךָ.
שַׂבְּעֵנוּ מִטּוּבֶךָ, וְשַׂמְּחֵנוּ בִּישׁוּעָתֶךָ, וְטַהֵר לִבֵּנוּ לְעָבְדְּךָ בֶּאֱמֶת.
וְהַנְחִילֵנוּ, יְיָ אֱלֹהֵינוּ, בְּאַהֲבָה וּבְרָצוֹן שַׁבַּת קָדְשֶׁךָ,
וְיָנוּחוּ בָהּ יִשְׂרָאֵל מְקַדְּשֵׁי שְׁמֶךָ. בָּרוּךְ אַתָּה יְיָ, מְקַדֵּשׁ הַשַּׁבָּת.

Shabbat Morning Service

• Our God and God of all Israel, grant that our worship on this Sabbath may be acceptable in Your sight. Sanctify us with Your Mitzvot that we may share in the blessings of Your word. Teach us to be satisfied with the gifts of Your goodness and gratefully to rejoice in all Your mercies. Purify our hearts that we may serve You in truth. O help us to preserve the Sabbath from generation to generation, that it may bring rest and joy, peace and comfort to the dwellings of our people, and through it Your name be hallowed in all the earth. We thank You, O God, for the Sabbath and its holiness.

❖ ❖

MOST PRECIOUS OF DAYS   יִשְׂמְחוּ

יִשְׂמְחוּ בְמַלְכוּתְךָ שׁוֹמְרֵי שַׁבָּת וְקוֹרְאֵי עֹנֶג. עַם מְקַדְּשֵׁי שְׁבִיעִי
כֻּלָּם יִשְׂבְּעוּ וְיִתְעַנְּגוּ מִטּוּבֶךָ. וְהַשְּׁבִיעִי רָצִיתָ בּוֹ וְקִדַּשְׁתּוֹ.
חֶמְדַּת יָמִים אוֹתוֹ קָרָאתָ, זֵכֶר לְמַעֲשֵׂה בְרֵאשִׁית.

Yis-m'chu v'ma-l'chu-t'cha sho-m'rei shabbat v'ko-r'ei o-neg. Am m'ka-d'shei sh'vi-i ku-lam yis-b'u v'yit-a-n'gu mi-tu-veh-cha. V'ha-sh'vi-i ra-tzi-ta vo v'ki-dash-toh. Chem-dat ya-mim o-toh ka-ra-ta, zei-cher l'ma-a-sei v'rei-sheet.

Those who keep the Sabbath and call it a delight shall rejoice in Your Presence. All who hallow the seventh day shall be gladdened by Your goodness. This day is Israel's festival of the spirit, sanctified and blessed by You, the most precious of days, a symbol of the joy of creation.

◆ ◆

Eternal God, establish this sanctuary, dedicated to Your holy name, so that the worship offered within its walls may be worthy of Your greatness and Your love. May every heart which seeks Your presence here find it, as did our people in the Temple on Zion, that this house may be a house of prayer for all peoples.

God our Creator, hear our prayer and bless us.

Have compassion upon all the house of Israel. Preserve us from sickness, from war, from strife. Keep us from hatred and uncharitableness toward our neighbors. And grant that, dwelling in safety and walking in uprightness, we may enjoy the fruit of our labors in peace.

God our Teacher, hear our prayer and bless us.

Be with all who spend themselves for the good of humanity and bear the burdens of others; who give bread to the hungry, clothe the naked, and provide shelter for the homeless. Establish, O God, the work of their hands, and grant them an abundant harvest of the good seed they are sowing.

God our Redeemer, hear our prayer and bless us.

Bless our children, O God, and help us so to fashion their souls by precept and example that they may ever love the good and turn from evil, revere Your Teaching and bring honor to their people. May they guard for future ages the truths revealed to our ancestors.

God our Friend, hear our prayer and bless us.

WORSHIP   עבודה

רְצֵה, יְיָ אֱלֹהֵֽינוּ, בְּעַמְּךָ יִשְׂרָאֵל, וּתְפִלָּתָם בְּאַהֲבָה תְקַבֵּל,

וּתְהִי לְרָצוֹן תָּמִיד עֲבוֹדַת יִשְׂרָאֵל עַמֶּֽךָ.

בָּרוּךְ אַתָּה יְיָ, שֶׁאוֹתְךָ לְבַדְּךָ בְּיִרְאָה נַעֲבוֹד.

O God, look with favor upon us, and may our service be acceptable to You. We praise You, Eternal One, whom alone we serve with reverence.

61

Shabbat Morning Service

MEDITATION

We give thanks for the freedom that is ours, and we pray for those in other lands who are persecuted and oppressed. Help them to bear their burdens and keep alive in them the love of freedom and the hope of deliverance. Uphold also the hands of our brothers and sisters in the land of Israel. Cause a new light to shine upon Zion and upon us all, that the time may come when Your Torah will go forth from the house of Israel, Your word from the tents of Jacob. We praise You, our God, whose presence gives life to our people Israel.

THANKSGIVING   הודאה

מוֹדִים אֲנַֽחְנוּ לָךְ, שָׁאַתָּה הוּא יְיָ אֱלֹהֵֽינוּ וֵאלֹהֵי אֲבוֹתֵֽינוּ
וְאִמּוֹתֵֽינוּ לְעוֹלָם וָעֶד. צוּר חַיֵּֽינוּ, מָגֵן יִשְׁעֵֽנוּ, אַתָּה הוּא
לְדוֹר וָדוֹר. נֽוֹדֶה לְּךָ וּנְסַפֵּר תְּהִלָּתֶֽךָ, עַל־חַיֵּֽינוּ הַמְּסוּרִים
בְּיָדֶֽךָ, וְעַל־נִשְׁמוֹתֵֽינוּ הַפְּקוּדוֹת לָךְ, וְעַל־נִסֶּֽיךָ שֶׁבְּכָל־יוֹם
עִמָּֽנוּ, וְעַל־נִפְלְאוֹתֶֽיךָ וְטוֹבוֹתֶֽיךָ שֶׁבְּכָל־עֵת, עֶֽרֶב וָבֹֽקֶר
וְצָהֳרָֽיִם. הַטּוֹב: כִּי לֹא־כָלוּ רַחֲמֶֽיךָ, וְהַמְרַחֵם: כִּי־לֹא תַֽמּוּ
חֲסָדֶֽיךָ, מֵעוֹלָם קִוִּֽינוּ לָךְ. וְעַל כֻּלָּם יִתְבָּרַךְ וְיִתְרוֹמַם שִׁמְךָ,
מַלְכֵּֽנוּ, תָּמִיד לְעוֹלָם וָעֶד. וְכֹל הַחַיִּים יוֹדֽוּךָ סֶּֽלָה, וִיהַלְלוּ
אֶת שִׁמְךָ בֶּאֱמֶת, הָאֵל יְשׁוּעָתֵֽנוּ וְעֶזְרָתֵֽנוּ סֶֽלָה. בָּרוּךְ אַתָּה
יְיָ, הַטּוֹב שִׁמְךָ וּלְךָ נָאֶה לְהוֹדוֹת.

* We gratefully acknowledge, Eternal God, that You are our Creator and Preserver, the Rock of our life and our protecting Shield.

We give thanks to You for our lives which are in Your hand, for our souls which are ever in Your keeping, for Your wondrous providence and Your continuous goodness, which You bestow upon us day by day. Truly, Your mercies never fail, and Your love and kindness never cease. Therefore do we put our trust in You. We praise You, Eternal One, to whom our thanks are due.

PEACE   בְּרְכַּת שָׁלוֹם

שִׂים שָׁלוֹם, טוֹבָה וּבְרָכָה, חֵן וָחֶסֶד וְרַחֲמִים, עָלֵינוּ
וְעַל־כָּל־יִשְׂרָאֵל וְעַל־כָּל־הָעַמִּים. בָּרְכֵנוּ אָבִינוּ, כֻּלָּנוּ כְּאֶחָד,
בְּאוֹר פָּנֶיךָ, כִּי בְאוֹר פָּנֶיךָ נָתַתָּ לָנוּ, יְיָ אֱלֹהֵינוּ,
תּוֹרַת חַיִּים וְאַהֲבַת חֶסֶד, וּצְדָקָה וּבְרָכָה וְרַחֲמִים,
וְחַיִּים וְשָׁלוֹם. וְטוֹב בְּעֵינֶיךָ לְבָרֵךְ אֶת־עַמְּךָ יִשְׂרָאֵל
וְאֶת־כָּל־הָעַמִּים בְּכָל־עֵת וּבְכָל־שָׁעָה בִּשְׁלוֹמֶךָ.
בָּרוּךְ אַתָּה יְיָ, עוֹשֵׂה הַשָּׁלוֹם.

° *Grant us peace, Your most precious gift, O Eternal Source of peace, and give us the will to proclaim its message to all the peoples of the earth.*

Bless our country, that it may always be a stronghold of peace, and its advocate among the nations.

May contentment reign within its borders, health and happiness within its homes.

Strengthen the bonds of friendship among the inhabitants of all lands, and may the love of Your name hallow every home and every heart. We praise You, Eternal One, Source of peace.

SILENT PRAYER
Psalm 15

יְהֹוָה, מִי־יָגוּר בְּאָהֳלֶךָ, מִי־יִשְׁכֹּן בְּהַר קָדְשֶׁךָ?
הוֹלֵךְ תָּמִים וּפֹעֵל צֶדֶק וְדֹבֵר אֱמֶת בִּלְבָבוֹ.
לֹא־רָגַל עַל־לְשֹׁנוֹ, לֹא־עָשָׂה לְרֵעֵהוּ רָעָה,
וְחֶרְפָּה לֹא־נָשָׂא עַל־קְרֹבוֹ.
נִבְזֶה בְּעֵינָיו נִמְאָס, וְאֶת־יִרְאֵי יְהֹוָה יְכַבֵּד.
נִשְׁבַּע לְהָרַע וְלֹא יָמִר.
כַּסְפּוֹ לֹא־נָתַן בְּנֶשֶׁךְ וְשֹׁחַד עַל־נָקִי לֹא לָקָח.
עֹשֵׂה־אֵלֶּה לֹא יִמּוֹט לְעוֹלָם.

Who may abide in Your house, O God?
Who may dwell in your holy mountain?

Those who are upright; who do justly;
who speak the truth within their hearts.

Who do not slander others, or wrong them,
or bring shame upon them.

Who give their word and, come what may, do not retract.
Who do not exploit others, who never take bribes.

Those who live in this way shall never be shaken.

◆ ◆

יִהְיוּ לְרָצוֹן אִמְרֵי־פִי וְהֶגְיוֹן לִבִּי לְפָנֶיךָ, יְהֹוָה, צוּרִי וְגֹאֲלִי.

May the words of my mouth, and the meditations of my heart, be
acceptable to You, O God, my Rock and my Redeemer.

◆

עֹשֶׂה שָׁלוֹם בִּמְרוֹמָיו, הוּא יַעֲשֶׂה שָׁלוֹם עָלֵינוּ
וְעַל־כָּל־יִשְׂרָאֵל, וְאִמְרוּ אָמֵן.

May the One who causes peace to reign in the high heavens let
peace descend on us, on all Israel, and all the world.

The Torah Service סדר קריאת התורה

אֵין־כָּמְוֹךָ בָאֱלֹהִים, אֲדֹנָי, וְאֵין כְּמַעֲשֶׂיךָ.

מַלְכוּתְךָ מַלְכוּת כָּל־עוֹלָמִים וּמֶמְשַׁלְתְּךָ בְּכָל־דּוֹר וָדוֹר.

יְהֹוָה מֶלֶךְ, יְהֹוָה מָלָךְ, יְהֹוָה יִמְלוֹךְ לְעוֹלָם וָעֶד.

יְהֹוָה עֹז לְעַמּוֹ יִתֵּן, יְהֹוָה יְבָרֵךְ אֶת־עַמּוֹ בַשָּׁלוֹם.

There is none like You, Eternal One, among the gods that are
worshipped, and there are no deeds like Yours. Your sovereignty
is everlasting; You reign through all generations.

God rules; God will reign for ever and ever. Eternal God, give
strength to Your people; Eternal God, bless Your people with
peace.

All rise

אֵל הָרַחֲמִים, הֵיטִיבָה בִרְצוֹנְךָ אֶת־צִיּוֹן;

תִּבְנֶה חוֹמוֹת יְרוּשָׁלָיִם.

כִּי בְךָ לְבַד בָּטָחְנוּ, מֶלֶךְ אֵל רָם וְנִשָּׂא, אֲדוֹן עוֹלָמִים.

Source of mercy, let Your goodness be a blessing to Zion; let
Jerusalem be rebuilt. In You alone do we trust, O Sovereign God,
high and exalted, Ruler of all the worlds.

The Ark is opened

הָבוּ גֹדֶל לֵאלֹהֵינוּ וּתְנוּ כָבוֹד לַתּוֹרָה.

Let us declare the greatness of our God and give honor
to the Torah.

Service for the reading of Torah

כִּי מִצִיּוֹן תֵּצֵא תוֹרָה, וּדְבַר־יְהֹוָה מִירוּשָׁלָיִם.
בָּרוּךְ שֶׁנָּתַן תּוֹרָה לְעַמּוֹ יִשְׂרָאֵל בִּקְדֻשָּׁתוֹ.

For out of Zion shall go forth Torah, and the word of God from
Jerusalem. Praised be the One who in holiness gives Torah to our
people Israel.

בֵּית יַעֲקֹב, לְכוּ וְנֵלְכָה בְּאוֹר יְהֹוָה:

O House of Israel, come, let us walk by the light of our God.

❖ ❖

שְׁמַע יִשְׂרָאֵל: יְהֹוָה אֱלֹהֵינוּ יְהֹוָה אֶחָד!
Sh'ma Yisrael, Adonai Ehloheinu, Adonai Echad!

Hear, O Israel: the Eternal One is our God,
the Eternal God alone!

אֶחָד אֱלֹהֵינוּ, גָּדוֹל אֲדֹנֵינוּ, קָדוֹשׁ שְׁמוֹ!
Echad Ehloheinu, gadol Adoneinu, kadosh sh'mo.

Our God is One; great and holy is the Eternal One.

❖ ❖

גַּדְּלוּ לַיהֹוָה אִתִּי, וּנְרוֹמְמָה שְׁמוֹ יַחְדָּו.

O magnify the Eternal One with me, and together let us exalt
God's name.

לְךָ, יְהֹוָה, הַגְּדֻלָּה וְהַגְּבוּרָה וְהַתִּפְאֶרֶת וְהַנֵּצַח וְהַהוֹד, כִּי כֹל
בַּשָּׁמַיִם וּבָאָרֶץ. לְךָ יְהֹוָה הַמַּמְלָכָה וְהַמִּתְנַשֵּׂא לְכֹל לְרֹאשׁ.

Yours, O God, is the greatness, the power, the glory, the victory,
and the majesty; for all that is in heaven and earth is Yours. You,
O God, are sovereign; You are supreme over all.

All are seated

Service for the reading of Torah

Before the reading

בָּרְכוּ אֶת־יְיָ הַמְבֹרָךְ!

בָּרוּךְ יְיָ הַמְבֹרָךְ לְעוֹלָם וָעֶד!

בָּרוּךְ אַתָּה יְיָ, אֱלֹהֵינוּ מֶלֶךְ הָעוֹלָם, אֲשֶׁר בָּחַר־בָּנוּ מִכָּל־
הָעַמִּים וְנָתַן־לָנוּ אֶת־תּוֹרָתוֹ. בָּרוּךְ אַתָּה יְיָ, נוֹתֵן הַתּוֹרָה.

READER: Ba-r'chu et Adonai ha-m'vo-rach!
CONGREGATION: Ba-ruch Adonai ha-m'vo-rach l'o-lam va-ed!
READER: Ba-ruch Adonai ha-m'vo-rach l'o-lam va-ed!
Ba-ruch a-ta Adonai, Ehloheinu mehlech ha-o-lam, a-sher ba-char
ba-nu mi-kol ha-a-mim, v'na-tan la-nu et Torah-toh. Ba-ruch a-ta
Adonai, no-tein ha-Torah.

Praise the One to whom praise is due!

Praised be the One to whom praise is due, now and for ever!

Praised be our Eternal God, Ruler of the universe, who has chosen us
from all peoples by giving us the Torah. We praise You, Eternal One,
Giver of the Torah.

After the Reading

בָּרוּךְ אַתָּה יְיָ, אֱלֹהֵינוּ מֶלֶךְ הָעוֹלָם, אֲשֶׁר נָתַן־לָנוּ תּוֹרַת
אֱמֶת וְחַיֵּי עוֹלָם נָטַע בְּתוֹכֵנוּ. בָּרוּךְ אַתָּה יְיָ, נוֹתֵן הַתּוֹרָה.

Ba-ruch a-ta Adonai, Ehloheinu mehlech ha-o-lam, a-sher na-tan
la-nu Toh-rat eh-met, v'cha-yei o-lam na-ta b'toh-chei-nu. Ba-ruch
a-ta Adonai, no-tein ha-Torah.

Praised be our Eternal God, Ruler of the universe, who has given us a
Torah of truth, implanting within us eternal life. We praise You, Eternal
One, Giver of the Torah.

*(As the reading is completed, the Torah might be held high, while
this is said or sung:)*

וְזֹאת הַתּוֹרָה אֲשֶׁר־שָׂם מֹשֶׁה לִפְנֵי בְּנֵי יִשְׂרָאֵל,

עַל־פִּי יְיָ בְּיַד־מֹשֶׁה.

This is the Torah that Moses placed before the people of Israel.

Service for the reading of Torah

Before the Reading

בָּרוּךְ אַתָּה יְיָ, אֱלֹהֵינוּ מֶלֶךְ הָעוֹלָם, אֲשֶׁר בָּחַר בִּנְבִיאִים
טוֹבִים וְרָצָה בְדִבְרֵיהֶם הַנֶּאֱמָרִים בֶּאֱמֶת.
בָּרוּךְ אַתָּה יְיָ, הַבּוֹחֵר בַּתּוֹרָה וּבְמֹשֶׁה עַבְדּוֹ
וּבְיִשְׂרָאֵל עַמּוֹ וּבִנְבִיאֵי הָאֱמֶת וָצֶדֶק.

Praised be our Eternal God, Ruler of the universe, who has called faithful prophets to speak words of truth. We praise You for the revelation of Torah, for Moses Your servant and Israel Your people, and for the prophets of truth and righteousness.

After the Reading
(An alternative version follows below)

בָּרוּךְ אַתָּה יְיָ, אֱלֹהֵינוּ מֶלֶךְ הָעוֹלָם,
צוּר כָּל־הָעוֹלָמִים, צַדִּיק בְּכָל־הַדּוֹרוֹת, הָאֵל הַנֶּאֱמָן,
הָאוֹמֵר וְעוֹשֶׂה, הַמְדַבֵּר וּמְקַיֵּם, שֶׁכָּל־דְּבָרָיו אֱמֶת וָצֶדֶק.

עַל־הַתּוֹרָה וְעַל־הָעֲבוֹדָה וְעַל־הַנְּבִיאִים וְעַל־יוֹם הַשַּׁבָּת
הַזֶּה, שֶׁנָּתַתָּ־לָּנוּ, יְיָ אֱלֹהֵינוּ, לִקְדֻשָּׁה וְלִמְנוּחָה, לְכָבוֹד
וּלְתִפְאָרֶת, עַל־הַכֹּל, יְיָ אֱלֹהֵינוּ, אֲנַחְנוּ מוֹדִים לָךְ
וּמְבָרְכִים אוֹתָךְ. יִתְבָּרַךְ שִׁמְךָ בְּפִי כָּל־חַי תָּמִיד
לְעוֹלָם וָעֶד. בָּרוּךְ אַתָּה יְיָ, מְקַדֵּשׁ הַשַּׁבָּת.

Praised be our Eternal God, Ruler of the universe, the Rock of all creation, the Righteous One of all generations, the faithful God whose word is deed, whose every command is just and true.

For the Torah, for the privilege of worship, for the prophets, and for this Shabbat that You, our Eternal God, have given us for holiness and rest, for honor and glory, we thank and praise You. May Your name be praised for ever by every living being. We praise You, Eternal One, for the Sabbath and its holiness.

Service for the reading of Torah

בָּרוּךְ אַתָּה יְיָ, אֱלֹהֵינוּ מֶלֶךְ הָעוֹלָם,
צוּר כָּל־הָעוֹלָמִים, צַדִּיק בְּכָל־הַדּוֹרוֹת, הָאֵל הַנֶּאֱמָן,
הָאוֹמֵר וְעוֹשֶׂה, הַמְדַבֵּר וּמְקַיֵּם, שֶׁכָּל־דְּבָרָיו אֱמֶת וָצֶדֶק.
נֶאֱמָן אַתָּה הוּא, יְיָ אֱלֹהֵינוּ, וְנֶאֱמָנִים דְּבָרֶיךָ, וְדָבָר אֶחָד
מִדְּבָרֶיךָ אָחוֹר לֹא־יָשׁוּב רֵיקָם, כִּי אֵל מֶלֶךְ נֶאֱמָן וְרַחֲמָן
אַתָּה. בָּרוּךְ אַתָּה יְיָ, הָאֵל הַנֶּאֱמָן בְּכָל־דְּבָרָיו.

רַחֵם עַל־צִיּוֹן, כִּי הִיא בֵּית חַיֵּינוּ, וְלָעֲלוּבַת נֶפֶשׁ תּוֹשִׁיעַ
בִּמְהֵרָה בְיָמֵינוּ. בָּרוּךְ אַתָּה יְיָ, מְשַׂמֵּחַ צִיּוֹן בְּבָנֶיהָ.

שַׂמְּחֵנוּ, יְיָ אֱלֹהֵינוּ, בְּאֵלִיָּהוּ הַנָּבִיא עַבְדֶּךָ, וּבְמַלְכוּת בֵּית
דָּוִד מְשִׁיחֶךָ: בִּמְהֵרָה יָבֹא וְיָגֵל לִבֵּנוּ. עַל־כִּסְאוֹ לֹא־יֵשֵׁב זָר,
וְלֹא־יִנְחֲלוּ עוֹד אֲחֵרִים אֶת־כְּבוֹדוֹ. כִּי בְשֵׁם קָדְשְׁךָ נִשְׁבַּעְתָּ
לּוֹ שֶׁלֹּא־יִכְבֶּה נֵרוֹ לְעוֹלָם וָעֶד. בָּרוּךְ אַתָּה יְיָ, מָגֵן דָּוִד.

עַל־הַתּוֹרָה וְעַל־הָעֲבוֹדָה וְעַל־הַנְּבִיאִים וְעַל־יוֹם הַשַּׁבָּת
הַזֶּה שֶׁנָּתַתָּ־לָּנוּ, יְיָ אֱלֹהֵינוּ, לִקְדֻשָּׁה וְלִמְנוּחָה, לְכָבוֹד
וּלְתִפְאָרֶת, עַל־הַכֹּל, יְיָ אֱלֹהֵינוּ, אֲנַחְנוּ מוֹדִים לָךְ
וּמְבָרְכִים אוֹתָךְ. יִתְבָּרַךְ שִׁמְךָ בְּפִי כָּל־חַי תָּמִיד
לְעוֹלָם וָעֶד. בָּרוּךְ אַתָּה יְיָ, מְקַדֵּשׁ הַשַּׁבָּת.

Praised be our Eternal God, Ruler of the universe, the Rock of all creation, the Righteous One of all generations, the faithful God whose word
is deed, whose every command is just and true.

You are the Faithful One, Eternal God, and faithful is Your word. Not
one word of Yours goes forth without accomplishing its task, O faithful
and compassionate One, Sovereign God. We praise You, Eternal One, the
faithful God.

Service for the reading of Torah

Show compassion for Zion, our House of Life, and banish all sadness speedily, in our own day. We praise You, Eternal One, who bring joy to Zion's children.

Eternal God, bring us the joy of Your sovereign rule: let our dream of Elijah and David bear fruit. Speedily let redemption come to gladden our hearts. Let Your solemn promise be fulfilled: David's light shall not for ever be extinguished! We praise You, Eternal One, Shield of David.

For the Torah, for the privilege of worship, for the prophets, and for this Shabbat that You, our Eternal God, have given us for holiness and rest, for honor and glory, we thank and praise You. May Your name be praised for ever by every living being. We praise You, Eternal One, for the Sabbath and its holiness.

Service for the reading of Torah

All rise

יְהַלְלוּ אֶת־שֵׁם יְהֹוָה, כִּי־נִשְׂגָּב שְׁמוֹ לְבַדּוֹ:

Let us praise the Eternal God, whose name alone is exalted.

◆

הוֹדוֹ עַל־אֶרֶץ וְשָׁמָיִם, וַיָּרֶם קֶרֶן לְעַמּוֹ,
תְּהִלָּה לְכָל־חֲסִידָיו, לִבְנֵי יִשְׂרָאֵל, עַם־קְרֹבוֹ. הַלְלוּיָהּ!

Your splendor covers heaven and earth; You are the strength of
Your people, making glorious Your faithful ones, Israel, a people
close to You. Halleluyah!

◆

תּוֹרַת יְהֹוָה תְּמִימָה, מְשִׁיבַת נָפֶשׁ;
עֵדוּת יְהֹוָה נֶאֱמָנָה, מַחְכִּימַת פֶּתִי.

God's Torah is perfect, reviving the soul;
God's teaching is sure, making wise the simple.

פִּקּוּדֵי יְהֹוָה יְשָׁרִים, מְשַׂמְּחֵי־לֵב;
מִצְוַת יְהֹוָה בָּרָה, מְאִירַת עֵינָיִם.

God's precepts are right, delighting the mind;
God's Mitzvah is clear, giving light to the eyes.

יִרְאַת יְהֹוָה טְהוֹרָה, עוֹמֶדֶת לָעַד;
מִשְׁפְּטֵי־יְהֹוָה אֱמֶת, צָדְקוּ יַחְדָּו.

God's word is pure, enduring for ever;
God's judgments are true, and altogether just.

◆

Behold, a good doctrine has been given you, My Torah; do not forsake it. It is a tree of life to those who hold it fast, and all who cling to it find happiness. Its ways are ways of pleasantness, and all its paths are peace.

כִּי לֶקַח טוֹב נָתַתִּי לָכֶם, תּוֹרָתִי אַל־תַּעֲזֹבוּ.

עֵץ־חַיִּים הִיא לַמַּחֲזִיקִים בָּהּ, וְתֹמְכֶיהָ מְאֻשָּׁר.

דְּרָכֶיהָ דַרְכֵי־נֹעַם, וְכָל־נְתִיבוֹתֶיהָ שָׁלוֹם.

Help us to return to You, O God; then truly shall we return. Renew our days as in the past.

הֲשִׁיבֵנוּ יְהוָה אֵלֶיךָ, וְנָשׁוּבָה. חַדֵּשׁ יָמֵינוּ כְּקֶדֶם.

The Ark is closed

All are seated

Aleinu I עלינו

All rise

עָלֵינוּ לְשַׁבֵּחַ לַאֲדוֹן הַכֹּל,
לָתֵת גְּדֻלָּה לְיוֹצֵר בְּרֵאשִׁית,
שֶׁלֹּא עָשָׂנוּ כְּגוֹיֵי הָאֲרָצוֹת,
וְלֹא שָׂמָנוּ כְּמִשְׁפְּחוֹת הָאֲדָמָה;
שֶׁלֹּא שָׂם חֶלְקֵנוּ כָּהֶם,
וְגוֹרָלֵנוּ כְּכָל־הֲמוֹנָם.
וַאֲנַחְנוּ כּוֹרְעִים וּמִשְׁתַּחֲוִים וּמוֹדִים לִפְנֵי
מֶלֶךְ מַלְכֵי הַמְּלָכִים, הַקָּדוֹשׁ בָּרוּךְ הוּא.

Aleinu l'sha-bei-ach la-a-don ha-kol, la-tet g'du-la l'yo-tzer b'rei-sheet, sheh-lo a-sa-nu k'go-yei ha-a-ra-tzot, v'lo sa-ma-nu k'mish-p'chot ha-a-da-ma; sheh-lo sam chel-kei-nu ka-hem, v'go-ra-lei-nu k'chol ha-mo-nam.
Va-a-nach-nu kor-im u-mish-ta-cha-vim u-mo-dim lif-nei me-lech mal-chei ha-m'la-chim, ha-ka-dosh ba-ruch hu.

We must praise the God of all, the Maker of heaven and earth, who has set us apart from the other families of earth, giving us a destiny unique among the nations.

Therefore we bow in awe and thanksgiving before the One who is sovereign over all, the Holy and Blessed One.

◆

שֶׁהוּא נוֹטֶה שָׁמַיִם וְיוֹסֵד אָרֶץ, וּמוֹשַׁב יְקָרוֹ בַּשָּׁמַיִם מִמַּעַל,
וּשְׁכִינַת עֻזּוֹ בְּגָבְהֵי מְרוֹמִים. הוּא אֱלֹהֵינוּ, אֵין עוֹד.
אֱמֶת מַלְכֵּנוּ, אֶפֶס זוּלָתוֹ, כַּכָּתוּב בְּתוֹרָתוֹ: "וְיָדַעְתָּ הַיּוֹם
וַהֲשֵׁבֹתָ אֶל־לְבָבֶךָ, כִּי יְיָ הוּא הָאֱלֹהִים בַּשָּׁמַיִם מִמַּעַל
וְעַל הָאָרֶץ מִתָּחַת, אֵין עוֹד."

You spread out the heavens and established the earth; You are our God; there is none else. In truth You alone are our sovereign God, as it is written: Know then this day and take it to heart: the Eternal One is God in the heavens above and on the earth below; there is none else.

עַל־כֵּן נְקַוֶּה לְךָ, יְיָ אֱלֹהֵינוּ, לִרְאוֹת מְהֵרָה בְּתִפְאֶרֶת עֻזֶּךָ,
לְהַעֲבִיר גִּלּוּלִים מִן הָאָרֶץ, וְהָאֱלִילִים כָּרוֹת יִכָּרֵתוּן,
לְתַקֵּן עוֹלָם בְּמַלְכוּת שַׁדַּי, וְכָל־בְּנֵי בָשָׂר יִקְרְאוּ בִשְׁמֶךָ,
לְהַפְנוֹת אֵלֶיךָ כָּל־רִשְׁעֵי אָרֶץ.

We therefore hope, our Eternal God, soon to behold the glory of Your might. Then will false gods vanish from our hearts, and the world be perfected under Your unchallenged rule. And then will all acclaim You as their God, and, forsaking evil, turn to You alone.

יַכִּירוּ וְיֵדְעוּ כָּל־יוֹשְׁבֵי תֵבֵל כִּי לְךָ תִּכְרַע כָּל־בֶּרֶךְ,
תִּשָּׁבַע כָּל־לָשׁוֹן. לְפָנֶיךָ, יְיָ אֱלֹהֵינוּ, יִכְרְעוּ וְיִפֹּלוּ,
וְלִכְבוֹד שִׁמְךָ יְקָר יִתֵּנוּ, וִיקַבְּלוּ כֻלָּם אֶת־עֹל מַלְכוּתֶךָ,
וְתִמְלֹךְ עֲלֵיהֶם מְהֵרָה לְעוֹלָם וָעֶד.

Let all who dwell on earth acknowledge that unto You every knee must bend and every tongue swear loyalty. Before You let them humble themselves. To Your glorious name let them give honor. Let all accept You as their Ruler, that You may reign over them soon and for ever.

כִּי הַמַּלְכוּת שֶׁלְּךָ הִיא, וּלְעוֹלְמֵי עַד תִּמְלוֹךְ בְּכָבוֹד.
כַּכָּתוּב בְּתוֹרָתֶךָ: "יְהֹוָה יִמְלֹךְ לְעֹלָם וָעֶד."

For You are sovereign, and to all eternity You will reign in glory, as it is written: God will reign for ever and ever.

וְנֶאֱמַר: "וְהָיָה יְהוָה לְמֶלֶךְ עַל־כָּל־הָאָרֶץ;
בַּיּוֹם הַהוּא יִהְיֶה יְהוָה אֶחָד וּשְׁמוֹ אֶחָד."

V'neh-eh-mar: V'ha-yah Adonai l'meh-lech al kol ha-a-retz;
ba-yom ha-hu yi-h'yeh Adonai echad, u-sh'mo echad!

And it has been said:
The Eternal God shall rule over all the earth;
On that day You shall be One and Your name shall be One.

Meditations before the Mourner's Kaddish begin on page 77

The Mourner's Kaddish is on page 78

Aleinu II עלינו

All rise

עָלֵינוּ לְשַׁבֵּחַ לַאֲדוֹן הַכֹּל,
לָתֵת גְּדֻלָּה לְיוֹצֵר בְּרֵאשִׁית,
שֶׁלֹּא עָשָׂנוּ כְּגוֹיֵי הָאֲרָצוֹת,
וְלֹא שָׂמָנוּ כְּמִשְׁפְּחוֹת הָאֲדָמָה;
שֶׁלֹּא שָׂם חֶלְקֵנוּ כָּהֶם,
וְגוֹרָלֵנוּ כְּכָל־הֲמוֹנָם.

° Let us adore the ever-living God! We render praise unto You who spread out the heavens and established the earth, whose glory is revealed in the heavens above, and whose greatness is manifest throughout the world. You are our God; there is none else.

וַאֲנַחְנוּ כּוֹרְעִים וּמִשְׁתַּחֲוִים וּמוֹדִים לִפְנֵי
מֶלֶךְ מַלְכֵי הַמְּלָכִים, הַקָּדוֹשׁ בָּרוּךְ הוּא.

Va-a-nach-nu kor-im u-mish-ta-cha-vim u-mo-dim lif-nei me-lech mal-chei ha-m'la-chim, ha-ka-dosh ba-ruch hu.

We therefore bow in awe and thanksgiving before the One who is Sovereign over all, the Holy and Blessed One.

All are seated

May the time not be distant, O God, when Your name shall be worshipped in all the earth, when unbelief shall disappear and error be no more. Fervently we pray that the day may come when all shall turn to You in love, when corruption and evil shall give way to integrity and goodness, when superstition shall no longer enslave the mind, nor idolatry blind the eye, when all who dwell on earth shall know that You alone are God. O may all, created in Your image, become one in spirit and one in friendship, for ever united in Your service. Then shall Your rule be established on earth, and the word of Your prophet fulfilled: The Eternal God will reign for ever and ever.

On that day, O God, You shall be One and Your name shall be One.

בַּיּוֹם הַהוּא יִהְיֶה יְהוָה אֶחָד וּשְׁמוֹ אֶחָד!
Ba-yom ha-hu yi-h'yeh Adonai echad, u-sh'mo echad!

76

Concluding Prayers

Our thoughts turn to those who have departed this earth: our own loved ones, those whom our friends and neighbors have lost, the martyrs of our people, and those of every race and nation whose lives have been a blessing to humanity. As we remember them, let us meditate on the meaning of love and loss, of life and death.

In Recent Grief

When cherished ties are broken, and the chain of love is shattered, only trust and the strength of faith can lighten the heaviness of the heart. At times, the pain of separation seems more than we can bear; but love and understanding can help us pass through the darkness toward the light.

Out of affliction the Psalmist learned the law of God. And in truth, grief is a great teacher, when it sends us back to serve and bless the living. We learn how to counsel and comfort those who, like ourselves, are bowed with sorrow. We learn when to keep silence in their presence, and when a word will assure them of our love and concern.

Thus, even when they are gone, the departed are with us, moving us to live as, in their higher moments, they themselves wished to live. We remember them now; they live in our hearts; they are an abiding blessing.

Strength for Those Who Mourn

In nature's ebb and flow, Your eternal law abides. As You are our support in the struggles of life, so, also, are You our hope in death. In Your care, O God, are the souls of all the living and the spirits of all flesh. Your power gives us strength; Your love comforts us. O Life of our life, Soul of our soul, cause Your light to shine into our hearts. Fill us with trust in You, and turn us again to the tasks of life. And may the memory of our loved ones inspire us to continue their work for the coming of Your sovereign rule.

Concluding Prayers

◆ ◆

We recall the loved ones whom death has recently taken from us . .
. And we remember those who died at this season in years past,
whom we have taken into our hearts with our own. The memories
of all of them are with us; our griefs and sympathies are mingled.
Loving God, we praise Your name:

MOURNER'S KADDISH   קדיש יתום

יִתְגַּדַּל וְיִתְקַדַּשׁ שְׁמֵהּ רַבָּא בְּעָלְמָא דִי־בְרָא כִרְעוּתֵהּ,
וְיַמְלִיךְ מַלְכוּתֵהּ בְּחַיֵּיכוֹן וּבְיוֹמֵיכוֹן וּבְחַיֵּי דְכָל־בֵּית יִשְׂרָאֵל,
בַּעֲגָלָא וּבִזְמַן קָרִיב, וְאִמְרוּ: אָמֵן.

Yit-ga-dal v'yit-ka-dash sh'mei ra-ba b'al-ma di-v'ra chir-u-tei,
v'yam-lich mal-chu-tei b'cha-yei-chon u-v'yo-mei-chon u-v'cha-yei
d'chol beit Yis-ra-el, ba-a-ga-la u-viz-man ka-riv, v'im-ru: A-mein.

יְהֵא שְׁמֵהּ רַבָּא מְבָרַךְ לְעָלַם וּלְעָלְמֵי עָלְמַיָּא.

Y'hei sh'mei ra-ba m'va-rach l'a-lam u-l'al-mei al-ma-ya.

יִתְבָּרַךְ וְיִשְׁתַּבַּח, וְיִתְפָּאַר וְיִתְרוֹמַם וְיִתְנַשֵּׂא, וְיִתְהַדָּר
וְיִתְעַלֶּה וְיִתְהַלָּל שְׁמֵהּ דְּקוּדְשָׁא, בְּרִיךְ הוּא,

Yit-ba-rach v'yish-ta-bach v'yit-pa-ar, v'yit-ro-mam, v'yit-na-sei,
v'yit-ha-dar, v'yit-a-leh, v'yit-ha-lal sh'mei d'kud'sha, b'rich hu,

לְעֵלָּא מִן־כָּל־בִּרְכָתָא וְשִׁירָתָא, תֻּשְׁבְּחָתָא וְנֶחֱמָתָא
דַּאֲמִירָן בְּעָלְמָא, וְאִמְרוּ: אָמֵן.

L'ei-la min kol bir-cha-ta v'shi-ra-ta, tush-b'cha-ta v'neh-cheh-ma-ta
da-a-mi-ran b'al-ma, v'im-ru: A-mein.

Concluding Prayers

יְהֵא שְׁלָמָא רַבָּא מִן־שְׁמַיָּא וְחַיִּים עָלֵינוּ וְעַל־כָּל־יִשְׂרָאֵל,
וְאִמְרוּ: אָמֵן.

Y'hei sh'la-ma ra-ba min sh'ma-ya v'cha-yim, a-lei-nu v'al kol Yis-ra-el, v'im-ru: A-mein.

עֹשֶׂה שָׁלוֹם בִּמְרוֹמָיו, הוּא יַעֲשֶׂה שָׁלוֹם עָלֵינוּ
וְעַל־כָּל־יִשְׂרָאֵל, וְאִמְרוּ: אָמֵן.

O-seh sha-lom bim-ro-mav, hu ya-a-seh sha-lom a-lei-nu v'al kol Yis-ra-el, v'im-ru: A-mein.

Let the glory of God be extolled, and God's great name be hallowed in the world whose creation God willed. May God rule in our own day, in our own lives, and in the life of all Israel, and let us say: Amen.

Let God's great name be blessed for ever and ever.

Beyond all the praises, songs, and adorations that we can utter is the Holy One, the Blessed One, whom yet we glorify, honor, and exalt. And let us say: Amen.

For us and for all Israel, may the blessing of peace and the promise of life come true, and let us say: Amen.

May the One who causes peace to reign in the high heavens, let peace descend on us, on all Israel, and all the world, and let us say: Amen.

◆

May the Source of peace send peace to all who mourn, and comfort to all who are bereaved. Amen.

Concluding Prayers

EVENING KIDDUSH   קדוש

Praised be our Eternal God, Ruler of the universe, Creator of the fruit of the vine.

Praised be our Eternal God, Ruler of the universe, for all the Mitzvot, and for the Mitzvah of Shabbat: the sign of Your love, a reminder of Your creative work, and of our liberation from Egyptian bondage, our day of days. On Shabbat we experience Your call to serve You as a holy people.

We praise You, Eternal One, for Shabbat and its holiness.

בָּרוּךְ אַתָּה יְיָ, אֱלֹהֵינוּ מֶלֶךְ הָעוֹלָם, בּוֹרֵא פְּרִי הַגָּפֶן.

בָּרוּךְ אַתָּה יְיָ, אֱלֹהֵינוּ מֶלֶךְ הָעוֹלָם, אֲשֶׁר קִדְּשָׁנוּ בְּמִצְוֹתָיו

וְרָצָה בָנוּ, וְשַׁבַּת קָדְשׁוֹ בְּאַהֲבָה וּבְרָצוֹן הִנְחִילָנוּ,

זִכָּרוֹן לְמַעֲשֵׂה בְרֵאשִׁית. כִּי הוּא יוֹם תְּחִלָּה לְמִקְרָאֵי קֹדֶשׁ,

זֵכֶר לִיצִיאַת מִצְרָיִם. כִּי־בָנוּ בָחַרְתָּ וְאוֹתָנוּ קִדַּשְׁתָּ

מִכָּל־הָעַמִּים, וְשַׁבַּת קָדְשְׁךָ בְּאַהֲבָה וּבְרָצוֹן הִנְחַלְתָּנוּ.

בָּרוּךְ אַתָּה יְיָ, מְקַדֵּשׁ הַשַּׁבָּת.

Ba-ruch a-ta A-do-nai, Eh-lo-hei-nu meh-lech ha-o-lam, bo-rei p'ri ha-ga-fen.

Ba-ruch a-ta A-do-nai, Eh-lo-hei-nu meh-lech ha-o-lam, a-sher ki-d'sha-nu b'mitz-vo-tav v'ra-tza va-nu, v'shabbat ko-d'sho b'a-ha-va u-v'ra-tzon hin-chi-la-nu, zi-ka-ron l'ma-a-sei v'rei-sheet. Ki hu yom t'chi-la l'mik-ra-ei ko-desh, zei-cher li-tzi-at Mitz-ra-yim.

Ki va-nu va-char-ta v'o-ta-nu ki-dash-ta mi-kol ha-a-mim, v'shabbat kod-sh'cha b'a-ha-va u-v'ra-tzon hin-chal-ta-nu. Ba-ruch a-ta A-do-nai, m'ka-deish ha-shabbat.

Concluding Prayers

MORNING KIDDUSH קדוש

וְשָׁמְרוּ בְנֵי־יִשְׂרָאֵל אֶת־הַשַּׁבָּת, לַעֲשׂוֹת אֶת־הַשַּׁבָּת לְדֹרֹתָם
בְּרִית עוֹלָם. בֵּינִי וּבֵין בְּנֵי יִשְׂרָאֵל אוֹת הִיא לְעֹלָם, כִּי־שֵׁשֶׁת
יָמִים עָשָׂה יְהוָה אֶת־הַשָּׁמַיִם וְאֶת־הָאָרֶץ, וּבַיּוֹם הַשְּׁבִיעִי
שָׁבַת וַיִּנָּפַשׁ.

V'sham'ru v'nei Yis-ra-el et ha-sha-bat, la-a-soht et ha-sha-bat
l'doh-ro-tam, b'rit o-lam. Bei-ni u-vein b'nei Yis-ra-el ot hi l'o-lam,
ki shei-shet ya-mim a-sa A-do-nai et ha-sha-ma-yim v'et ha-a-rets,
u-va-yom ha-sh'vi-i sha-vat va-yi-na-fash.

The people of Israel shall keep the Sabbath, observing the Sabbath
in every generation as a covenant for all time. It is a sign for ever
between Me and the people of Israel, for in six days the Eternal
God made heaven and earth, taking rest and refreshment on the
seventh day.

עַל־כֵּן בֵּרַךְ יְהוָה אֶת־יוֹם הַשַּׁבָּת וַיְקַדְּשֵׁהוּ.

Al kein bei-rach Adonai et yom ha-shabbat va-y'ka-d'shei-hu.

Therefore the Eternal One blessed the seventh day and called it
holy.

בָּרוּךְ אַתָּה יְיָ, אֱלֹהֵינוּ מֶלֶךְ הָעוֹלָם, בּוֹרֵא פְּרִי הַגָּפֶן.

Ba-ruch a-ta Adonai, Eh-lo-hei-nu meh-lech ha-o-lam, bo-rei p'ri
ha-ga-fen.

Praised be our Eternal God, Ruler of the universe, Creator of the
fruit of the vine.

82

Songs

אדון עולם

אֲדוֹן עוֹלָם אֲשֶׁר מָלַךְ, בְּטֶרֶם כָּל־יְצִיר נִבְרָא,
לְעֵת נַעֲשָׂה בְחֶפְצוֹ כֹּל, אֲזַי מֶלֶךְ שְׁמוֹ נִקְרָא.

A-don o-lam, a-sher ma-lach b'teh-rem kol y'tzir niv-ra,
L'eit na-a-sa v'chef-tzo kol, a-zai meh-lech sh'mo nik-ra.

וְאַחֲרֵי כִּכְלוֹת הַכֹּל, לְבַדּוֹ יִמְלֹךְ נוֹרָא,
וְהוּא הָיָה וְהוּא הֹוֶה, וְהוּא יִהְיֶה בְּתִפְאָרָה.

V'a-cha-rei kich-loht ha-kol, l'va-doh yim-loch no-ra,
V'hu ha-ya, v'hu ho-veh, v'hu yi-h'yeh b'tif-a-ra.

וְהוּא אֶחָד וְאֵין שֵׁנִי, לְהַמְשִׁיל לוֹ, לְהַחְבִּירָה,
בְּלִי רֵאשִׁית, בְּלִי תַכְלִית, וְלוֹ הָעֹז וְהַמִּשְׂרָה.

V'hu eh-chad, v'ein shei-ni l'ham-shil lo, l'hach-bi-ra,
B'li rei-sheet, b'li tach-lit, v'lo ha-oz v'ha-mis-ra.

וְהוּא אֵלִי וְחַי גֹּאֲלִי, וְצוּר חֶבְלִי בְּעֵת צָרָה,
וְהוּא נִסִּי וּמָנוֹס לִי, מְנָת כּוֹסִי בְּיוֹם אֶקְרָא.

V'hu ei-li, v'chai go-a-li, v'tzur chev-li b'eit tza-ra,
V'hu ni-si u-ma-nos li, m'nat ko-si b'yom ek-ra.

בְּיָדוֹ אַפְקִיד רוּחִי, בְּעֵת אִישַׁן וְאָעִירָה,
וְעִם רוּחִי גְּוִיָּתִי, יְיָ לִי וְלֹא אִירָא.

B'ya-doh af-kid ru-chi, b'eit i-shan v'a-i-ra,
V'im ru-chi g'vi-ya-ti, a-do-nai li, v'lo i-ra.

You are the Eternal God, who reigned before any being had been created;
when all was done according to Your will, already then you were Sovereign. And after all has ceased to be, still will You reign in solitary majesty;
You were, You are, You will be in glory. And You are One; none other
can compare to You, or consort with You; You are without beginning,

without end; Yours alone are power and dominion. And You are my God, my living Redeemer, my Rock in time of trouble and distress; You are my banner and my refuge, my benefactor when I call on You. Into Your hands I entrust my spirit, when I sleep and when I wake; my body also: You are with me, I shall not fear.

אין כאלהינו

אֵין כֵּאלֹהֵינוּ,	Ein kei-lo-hei-nu,
אֵין כַּאדוֹנֵינוּ,	ein ka-doh-nei-nu,
אֵין כְּמַלְכֵּנוּ,	ein k'mal-kei-nu,
אֵין כְּמוֹשִׁיעֵנוּ.	ein k'moh-shi-ein-u.

There is none like our God, our Sovereign, our Redeemer.

מִי כֵאלֹהֵינוּ?	Mi chei-lo-hei-nu?
מִי כַאדוֹנֵינוּ?	mi cha-doh-nei-nu?
מִי כְמַלְכֵּנוּ?	mi ch'mal-kei-nu?
מִי כְמוֹשִׁיעֵנוּ?	mi ch'moh-shi-ei-nu?

Who is like our God, our Sovereign, our Redeemer?

נוֹדֶה לֵאלֹהֵינוּ,	No-deh lei-lo-hei-nu,
נוֹדֶה לַאדוֹנֵינוּ,	no-deh la-doh-nei-nu,
נוֹדֶה לְמַלְכֵּנוּ,	no-deh l'mal-kei-nu,
נוֹדֶה לְמוֹשִׁיעֵנוּ.	no-deh l'moh-shi-ei-nu.

We give thanks to our God, our Sovereign, our Redeemer.

בָּרוּךְ אֱלֹהֵינוּ,	Ba-ruch Eh-lo-hei-nu,
בָּרוּךְ אֲדוֹנֵינוּ,	ba-ruch A-doh-nei-nu,
בָּרוּךְ מַלְכֵּנוּ,	ba-ruch mal-kei-nu,
בָּרוּךְ מוֹשִׁיעֵנוּ.	ba-ruch moh-shi-ei-nu.

Praised be our God, our Sovereign, our Redeemer.

Songs

אַתָּה הוּא אֱלֹהֵינוּ,
a-ta hu Eh-lo-hei-nu,

אַתָּה הוּא אֲדוֹנֵינוּ,
a-ta hu A-doh-nei-nu,

אַתָּה הוּא מַלְכֵּנוּ,
a-ta hu mal-kei-nu,

אַתָּה הוּא מוֹשִׁיעֵנוּ.
a-ta hu moh-shi-ei-nu.

You alone are our God, our Sovereign, our Redeemer.

יגדל

1 יִגְדַּל אֱלֹהִים חַי וְיִשְׁתַּבַּח, נִמְצָא וְאֵין עֵת אֶל־מְצִיאוּתוֹ.
אֶחָד וְאֵין יָחִיד כְּיִחוּדוֹ, נֶעְלָם וְגַם אֵין סוֹף לְאַחְדּוּתוֹ.

Yigdal Elohim chai v'yish-ta-bach, nim-tza v'ein eit el m'tzi-u-toh.
Echad, v'ein ya-chid, k'yi-chu-do, neh-lam v'gam ein sof l'ach-
du-toh.

Magnified be the living God, praised, whose existence is eternal, One and
Unique in that unity, the unfathomable One whose Oneness is infinite.

2 אֵין לוֹ דְמוּת הַגּוּף וְאֵינוֹ גוּף, לֹא נַעֲרוֹךְ אֵלָיו קְדֻשָּׁתוֹ.
קַדְמוֹן לְכָל־דָּבָר אֲשֶׁר נִבְרָא, רִאשׁוֹן וְאֵין רֵאשִׁית לְרֵאשִׁיתוֹ.

Ein lo d'mut ha-guf, v'ei-no guf, lo na-a-roch ei-lav k'du-sha-toh.
Kad-mon l'chol da-var a-sher niv-ra, ri-shon v'ein rei-sheet
l'rei-shi-toh.

A God with no bodily form, incorporeal, whose holiness is beyond compare, who preceded all creation, the Beginning who has no beginning!

3 הִנּוֹ אֲדוֹן עוֹלָם לְכָל־נוֹצָר, יוֹרֶה גְדֻלָּתוֹ וּמַלְכוּתוֹ.
שֶׁפַע נְבוּאָתוֹ נְתָנוֹ, אֶל־אַנְשֵׁי סְגֻלָּתוֹ וְתִפְאַרְתּוֹ.

Hi-no a-don o-lam, l'chol no-tzar, yo-reh g'du-la-toh u-mal-
chu-toh. Sheh-fa n'vu-a-toh n'ta'noh el an-shei s'gu-la-toh
v'tif-ar-toh.

You are Eternal Might, who teach every creature Your greatness and sovereignty, with the gift of prophecy inspiring those to whom You choose
to make Your glory known.

85

4   לֹא קָם בְּיִשְׂרָאֵל כְּמֹשֶׁה עוֹד נָבִיא וּמַבִּיט אֶת־תְּמוּנָתוֹ,
תּוֹרַת אֱמֶת נָתַן לְעַמּוֹ אֵל, עַל יַד נְבִיאוֹ נֶאֱמַן בֵּיתוֹ.

Lo kam b'yis-ra-el k'mo-sheh ohd na-vi u-ma-bit et t'mu-na-toh,
Toh-rat eh-met na-tan l'a-mo eil, al yad n'vi-o neh-man bei-toh.

Never has there been a prophet like Moses, whose closeness to You is
unmatched. A Torah of truth You gave Your people through Your
prophet, Your faithful servant.

5   לֹא יַחֲלִיף הָאֵל, וְלֹא יָמִיר דָּתוֹ, לְעוֹלָמִים לְזוּלָתוֹ.
צוֹפֶה וְיוֹדֵעַ סְתָרֵינוּ, מַבִּיט לְסוֹף דָּבָר בְּקַדְמָתוֹ.

Lo ya-cha-lif ha-eil, v'lo ya-mir da-toh, l'o-la-mim l'zu-la-toh.
Tzo-feh v'yo-dei-a s'ta-rei-nu, ma-bit l'sof da-var b'kad-ma-toh.

A changeless God, ever the same, whose teaching will stand, who watches
us and knows our inmost thoughts, who knows all outcomes before events
begin!

6   גּוֹמֵל לְאִישׁ חֶסֶד כְּמִפְעָלוֹ, נוֹתֵן לְרָשָׁע רַע כְּרִשְׁעָתוֹ.
יִשְׁלַח לְקֵץ יָמִין פְּדוּת עוֹלָם, כָּל־חַי וְיֵשׁ יַכִּיר יְשׁוּעָתוֹ.

Go-meil l'ish cheh-sed k'mif-a-lo, no-tein l'ra-sha ra k'rish-a-toh.
Yish-lach l'keitz ya-min p'dut o-lam, kol chai v'yeish ya-kir
y'shu-a-toh.

You give us each what we deserve, the good and bad alike. In the end of
days You will send an everlasting redemption; all that lives and has being
shall witness Your deliverance.

7   חַיֵּי עוֹלָם נָטַע בְּתוֹכֵנוּ, בָּרוּךְ עֲדֵי עַד שֵׁם תְּהִלָּתוֹ.

Cha-yei o-lam na-ta b'toh-chei-nu, ba-ruch a-dei ad sheim
t'hi-la-toh.

You have implanted eternal life within us; praised be Your glory to all
eternity!

Songs

שָׁלוֹם עֲלֵיכֶם

שָׁלוֹם עֲלֵיכֶם, מַלְאֲכֵי הַשָּׁרֵת, מַלְאֲכֵי עֶלְיוֹן,
מִמֶּלֶךְ מַלְכֵי הַמְּלָכִים, הַקָּדוֹשׁ בָּרוּךְ הוּא.

Sha-lom a-lei-chem mal-a-chei ha-sha-reit, mal-a-chei el-yon,
Mi-meh-lech mal-chei ha-m'la-chim, ha-ka-dosh ba-ruch hu.

בּוֹאֲכֶם לְשָׁלוֹם, מַלְאֲכֵי הַשָּׁלוֹם, מַלְאֲכֵי עֶלְיוֹן,
מִמֶּלֶךְ מַלְכֵי הַמְּלָכִים, הַקָּדוֹשׁ בָּרוּךְ הוּא.

Bo-a-chem l'sha-lom, mal-a-chei ha-sha-lom, mal-a-chei el-yon,
Mi-meh-lech mal-chei ha-m'la-chim, ha-ka-dosh ba-ruch hu.

בָּרְכוּנִי לְשָׁלוֹם, מַלְאֲכֵי הַשָּׁלוֹם, מַלְאֲכֵי עֶלְיוֹן,
מִמֶּלֶךְ מַלְכֵי הַמְּלָכִים, הַקָּדוֹשׁ בָּרוּךְ הוּא.

Ba-r'chu-ni l'sha-lom, mal-a-chei ha-sha-lom, mal-a-chei el-yon,
Mi-meh-lech mal-chei ha-m'la-chim, ha-ka-dosh ba-ruch hu.

צֵאתְכֶם לְשָׁלוֹם, מַלְאֲכֵי הַשָּׁלוֹם, מַלְאֲכֵי עֶלְיוֹן,
מִמֶּלֶךְ מַלְכֵי הַמְּלָכִים, הַקָּדוֹשׁ בָּרוּךְ הוּא.

Tzei-t'chem l'sha-lom, mal-a-chei ha-sha-lom, mal-a-chei el-yon,
Mi-meh-lech mal-chei ha-m'la-chim, ha-ka-dosh ba-ruch hu.

Peace be to you, O ministering angels, messengers of the Most High, from the supreme Sovereign, the Holy One, the Blessed One.

Enter in peace, O messengers of peace, messengers of the Most High, from the supreme Sovereign, the Holy One, the Blessed One.

Bless me with peace, O messengers of peace, messengers of the Most High, from the supreme Sovereign, the Holy One, the Blessed One.

Depart in peace, O messengers of peace, messengers of the Most High, from the supreme Sovereign, the Holy One, the Blessed One.

שבת המלכה

הַחַמָּה מֵרֹאשׁ הָאִילָנוֹת נִסְתַּלְּקָה,
בְּאוּ וְנֵצֵא לִקְרַאת שַׁבָּת הַמַּלְכָּה.
הִנֵּה הִיא יוֹרֶדֶת, הַקְּדוֹשָׁה הַבְּרוּכָה.
וְעִמָּהּ מַלְאָכִים, צְבָא שָׁלוֹם וּמְנוּחָה.
בֹּאִי בֹּאִי הַמַּלְכָּה!
בֹּאִי בֹּאִי הַכַּלָּה!
שָׁלוֹם עֲלֵיכֶם מַלְאֲכֵי הַשָּׁלוֹם.

The sun on the treetops no longer is seen,
Come gather to welcome the Sabbath, our queen.
Behold her descending, the holy, the blessed,
And with her the angels of peace and of rest.
Draw near, draw near, and here abide,
Draw near, draw near, O Sabbath bride.
Peace also to you, you angels of peace.

COME, O SABBATH DAY

Come, O Sabbath day and bring
Peace and healing on your wing;
And to every weary one
Let your word of blessing come:
You shall rest, You shall rest.

Welcome Sabbath, let depart
Every care of troubled heart;
Now the daily task is done,
Let your word of comfort come:
You shall rest, You shall rest.

Wipe from ev'ry cheek the tear,
Banish care and silence fear;
All hearts turning to the best,
Teach us the divine behest:
You shall rest, You shall rest.

Songs

O HOLY SABBATH DAY

O holy Sabbath day, draw near,
You are the source of bliss and cheer;
The first in God's creative thought,
The final aim of all God wrought.
   Welcome, welcome, day of rest,
   Day of joy that God has blessed.

Let all rejoice with all their might,
The Sabbath, freedom brings and light;
Let songs of praise to God ascend,
And voices sweet in chorus blend.
   Welcome, welcome, day of rest,
   Day of joy that God has blessed.

Now come, O blessed Sabbath-Bride,
Our joy, our comfort, and our pride;
All cares and sorrow now bid cease,
And fill our waiting hearts with peace.
   Welcome, welcome, day of rest,
   Day of joy that God has blessed.

COME, O HOLY SABBATH EVENING

Come, O holy Sabbath evening,
Crown our toil with well earned rest;
Bring us hallowed hours of gladness,
Day of days beloved and blest.

Weave your mystic spell around us
With the glow of Sabbath light:
As we read the ancient wisdom,
Learn its laws of truth and right.

Come, O holy Sabbath spirit,
Radiant shine from every eye;
Lending us your benediction,
Filling every heart with joy.

Songs

אשא עיני

<table>
<tr>
<td dir="rtl">

אֶשָּׂא עֵינַי אֶל הֶהָרִים,

מֵאַיִן יָבֹא עֶזְרִי.

עֶזְרִי מֵעִם יְהוָֹה,

עֹשֵׂה שָׁמַיִם וָאָרֶץ.

</td>
<td>

Eh-sa ei-nai el heh-ha-rim,

mei-ah-yin ya-voh ez-ri.

Ez-ri mei-im Adonai,

o-seh sha-ma-yim va-a-retz.

</td>
</tr>
</table>

I lift up my eyes, unto the mountains,
Where, oh where, will I find my help?
My help will come from my God,
Maker of heaven and earth.